A FIRESIDE BOOK
PUBLISHED BY SIMON & SCHUSTER

NEW YORK   LONDON   TORONTO   SYDNEY   SINGAPORE

My Mother, My Friend

*The Ten Most Important Things
to Talk About with Your Mother*

Mary Marcdante

Fireside

Rockefeller Center

1230 Avenue of the Americas

New York, NY 10020

Copyright © 2001 by Mary Marcdante

All rights reserved,

including the right of reproduction

in whole or in part in any form.

FIRESIDE and colophon are registered trademarks

of Simon & Schuster, Inc.

Designed by Diane Hobbing

Manufactured in the United States of America

1 3 5 7 9 10 8 6 4 2

Library of Congress Cataloging-in-Publication Data

Marcdante, Mary.

My mother, my friend : the ten most important things to talk
about with your mother / Mary Marcdante.

p. cm.

1. Mothers and daughters.   2. Communication in the family.

3. Aging parents—Family relationships.   I. Title.

HQ755.86 .M37 2001

306.874'3—dc21   00-051012

ISBN 0-684-86606-4 (pbk.)

ACKNOWLEDGMENTS

Of all the writing I have done on this book, these acknowledgment pages are the most meaningful to me for, without the people mentioned here, this book would still be a dream. I have often heard that writing a book is a team project, but I never anticipated that I would be graced with such a jubilant, loving, and encouraging band of angels:

Laurie Fox, my guardian angel, friend, and agent, who believed in me and my ability to write before I did and held my hand through this entire journey. Linda Chester for saying yes and calling me personally to express her pleasure that her agency was representing me as an author. My editor, Caroline Sutton, for her grace, integrity, insight, and attention, and for bringing my mother's most precious qualities back to life. The team at Simon & Schuster/Fireside for embracing this book so completely and thoughtfully.

My partner, John Kalpus, for his love, humor, music, unending support, and willingness to listen again and again to my one-track "mother" mind over the past three years. My father, Bob Sherburne, now deceased, for showing me that love can teach an old dog new tricks, and for giving me a love of words and the arts. My siblings, Jeanne Sherer, Paul Sherburne, and Eileen Sherburne, for letting me tell my version of our family story and for their loyalty and commitment to keeping our family together since Mom and Dad died. My tribe of nephews, Tom, Michael, Jimmy, Holden, and Joe, for their laughter and curiosity and learning to ask with every phone call, "How is your book coming along, Auntie Mary?" My godmother, Dorothy, and my mother's other two sisters, Marian and Bernice, for their memories and their laughter that sounds just like Mom's. My extended family of aunts, uncles, and cousins, especially Sister Francile Sherburne for her English language and creative writing influence, Father Richard Sherburne and Brother Basil Rothweiler for their spiritual guidance, and Jane Sherburne, Cile Smith, Chris Wiencke, and JoAnne Trammel for their memories and encouragement while I was writing.

My always-there-when-I-need-them friends, Roxanne Emmerich, Dianne Gardner, Debbie Harvey-Aiken, Holly Herman, Kate Larsen, Patti Lechmaier, Mary Jane Mapes, Barbara Markoff, Lori Neustedter, Nicole Petzolt, Christine Phinney, Nancy Stern, and Jeanne Sherer, for their love and their stories, and for letting me read pages and pages of my writing to them without interrupting me. My walking buddies, Kim Piker, Mo Rafael, and Liz Livingston, for keeping my body moving as well as my mind. Rosita Perez for starting me on the road to understanding my mother. Leslie Charles for being there whenever I needed her and passing on her author wisdom and encouragement. Mary LoVerde for walking the talk of truth, love, and trust with me. Susan RoAne for always having something practical and pithy to offer in response to my questions and making me think like a best-selling author. Marci Shimoff for asking me to write my story for her Chicken Soup book. Sheryl Roush for taking a weeklong speaking tour so I could finish my proposal. Chris Clark-Epstein for being the very wise big sister I always wanted and her mother, June Blomberg, for being my virtual email mother. Annie and David Duval for their meals, energy, and conversation when I was too tired to cook.

Mary Rice for planting seeds of feminine strength in me, helping me break through my writing blocks, and sharing her wonderful mother Edith Leech with me. Mimi Miller for her healing acupuncture. Lynn Greenberg, Christine Harris, Louise Hay, Jean Hermsen, Alexandra Kennedy, Harriet Lerner, Suze Orman, Stella Resnick, Geneen Roth, Marilyn Solomon, Virginia Satir, Myra Mae Von Uxem, and Oprah Winfrey for reminding me that I am allowed to be a strong, confident, independent woman, worthy of love and respect.

The National Speakers Association for providing the structure, leadership training, mentors, and friends, including Dan Burrus, Mary-Ellen Drummond, Elizabeth Jeffries, Susan Page, Lesa Heebner, Sam Horn, Lael Jackson, Terri Lonier, Joan Lloyd, Nanci McGraw, Sheila Paxton, Naomi Rhode, Lorna Riley, Nancy Rosanoff, Jane Sanders, Barbara Sanfilippo, Marilynn Semonick, Stephen Tweed, and George Walther, whose stories, insight, phone calls, and e-mails kept me focused and connected during my writing sabbatical. Mount Mary College and National Association for Women's Health for their enthusiastic support of me and their commitment to women's well-being. Beverly Weurding for her enthusiasm and friendship, and for hiring me repeatedly. Hope Edelman for having coffee with me and telling me my book was needed in the world. Betsy Rapoport for renewing the momentum that brought me to New York. Catherine Bradford and Judith Estrine for their editing skill and helping me find my writing voice. Nicole Diamond, Loretta Denner, and Beverly Miller for their attention to details and keeping me on track. Marilyn Davies for her photography and joy. Ron Sobel for his legal advice regarding song titles. Joel Roberts and Nancy Greystone for their superb media training.

Judy Hacker at *Momversations.com*, Lenore Howe at *wellnessweb.com*, Marilyn Krebs, Carol Krause at the Office on Women's Health, Jane Sarasota-Kahn, and Lillie Shockney at *mothersdaughters.org* for sharing their expertise without hesitation.

All the women in my seminars, friends, and friends of friends, some who chose to remain anonymous, all who offered questions, were willing to be interviewed and share their stories of healing and celebration whether or not they were printed. Thank you for your generous spirit, which flows through every page of this book.

In memory of Frances Kalpus, Diane Kalpus Schmidt, and Farley Meowcat Kalpus, whose lives and deaths during this journey remind me of how important our presence is to each other, especially when it seems least apparent.

And to God for all the miracles I've witnessed and the faith I can no longer deny. I am so blessed. Thank you.

In celebration of my mother

GRACE ROSE ROTHWEILER SHERBURNE

CONTENTS

PREFACE

At what point do a mother and daughter decide that they can come together as one friend to another? For some women it's after they have married. For others, it is the birth of their first child, and still some others, it is during a physical or emotional crisis.

For me, it was the diagnosis of my mother's ovarian cancer. From the moment I heard she had cancer until her death, I felt as if I was in graduate school, cramming the night before finals for a course called, "Everything You've Always Wanted to Know About Your Mother and Forgot to Ask."

Following her death, there were still so many unanswered questions that neither my father nor her sisters nor her friends were able to answer. I began talking with women in my audiences (I am a professional speaker at conventions, business meetings, and women's conferences) about their relationships with their mothers and learned that most women (and men) have questions they want to ask their mothers. Even more surprising was that many women have unfinished business with their mothers and are afraid to broach certain subjects. I was curious to learn more about this phenomenon.

In pursuit of answers, I interviewed psychologists and psychotherapists, read feminist essays, revisited my own past, and kept talking to women in my seminars. I learned that all too often a mature woman relates to her mother the way she did when she was an adolescent. She locks her mother into one role—that of "mother"—and is unable to see her as a dynamic, multifaceted person in her own right—the way she would a friend. This prevents her from knowing her mother at a deeper and more satisfying level and discovering more about herself.

Questions are the beginning of discovery. As I became more immersed in this work, I woke before dawn one morning from a dream in which my mother suggested I write a book of questions that daughters could ask their mothers. I was excited by the concept but unsure how viable it was, so I took the idea to the women in my programs. Their response was overwhelmingly positive. When I asked these women what questions they wanted to ask their mothers, I received hundreds at each program, covering every area in a woman's life. The list revealed many insights but one in particular caught my attention. Every daughter has at least one burning question that she is afraid to ask her mother—and may not even be aware of until she's thrown into a crisis situation, as was the case with me. Once I knew that Mom's death was imminent, it took me a month to find the courage and right time to ask, "Mom, how do you *really* feel about dying?" When I finally did ask, her answer was so enlightening and affirming that I couldn't believe I waited so long to approach her.

My success was due in large part to learning and repeatedly practicing the skills I'll be sharing in this book—the first skill being to pay attention to your mother in a new way. My mother's illness—while I don't wish it on anyone—was a gift that allowed me to begin seeing her with fresh eyes. I learned to let in more of her love, wisdom, and humor and accept the fact that she wasn't ever going to be like TV's perfect mothers I grew up comparing her to—June Cleaver, Donna Reed, and Harriet Nelson. I only wish I'd been able to do this sooner, as you'll be able to with this book.

Some women in my audiences have said, "Easy for you to say! Your mother is gone. I still have to deal with mine." True, I can't argue that. *And* the time my mother and I did share before she died included many significant question-and-answer sessions. In turn, there are hundreds of women whose mothers are still alive who have successfully used the material in this book. Many are profiled here. They show by example that a daughter can have a healthier and more satisfying relationship with her mom. All you have to do to begin is start thinking of your mother as a friend you'd like to get to know better. If this is challenging for you, consider my story.

I by no means identified with my mother as a friend; she was "just" my mother. The funny thing is that when I was writing this book, it became very clear to me that although I wouldn't have said that my mother and I were friends, our actions told the truth. We laughed together, cheered each other up, talked about things that were important, and cared about each other's well-being. We did things that friends do—only I didn't think we were friends. I'd grown up believing that mothers aren't supposed to be friends with their daughters.

In my mother's generation, a mother's role was solely to guide and protect, not to share her personal experiences or problems the way a dear friend would. It was taboo for a mother to tell her daughter that she felt depressed or afraid, or even admit that she was proud of herself. This would be considered too frank and personal; her daughter might not be able to handle it. Based on my personal experience and research, a balance must be struck with young daughters: age-appropriate truth telling established with a clear boundary that says, "I'm the mom." But once a woman reaches adulthood, an added benefit of having a mother is the potential for friendship. The opportunity to exchange thoughts and intimate feelings helps both women explore solutions to problems and ask and answer difficult or meaningful questions about life.

My friend Barbara says that her relationship with her mother goes beyond friendship. Barbara defines her friends as people with whom she shares common interests and does things with socially. "My mother is more than a friend," Barbara said. "She's my *mother*. I call her first with any big news—good or bad. I expect her to be there when I'm in crisis. When I'm sick, I want her to take care of me. It's so much more than friendship."

However you choose to view your mother, ask yourself these questions: Do I see my mother for all she is and can be? What parts of her would I want to know more about? What would help us be closer? What would take our relationship to a new level?

Even if you don't want to be the best of friends with your mother, you can still work on creating a richer relationship. If your situation is reversed and you think your mother doesn't want to have a deeper relationship with you, keep reading anyway. There is always a possibility that she will choose not to be close to you. Then again, there's always the chance that she will come around after seriously considering a request on your part to get to know her better. If you believe she isn't interested based on your past history, please talk to her first, using the ideas and words in this book. If, once you've spoken with your mother, she is still resistant and it's still important to you to know her better, don't give up. Hold a space in your heart for your mother to change. You may be surprised by the result, as Linda, whom you'll meet in the Introduction, was. Even if your mother never desires a more intimate relationship, go about making your life as joyful as possible so that you are still taking care of yourself. If she does open up to you, you'll be ready to embrace her in love and forgiveness. If your mother has passed on, by reading the stories and reviewing the questions, you'll draw out precious memories that will help you heal your loss, as writing this book did for me.

What's the Best Way to Use This Book?

Twenty topics surfaced as this book took form, with ten topics being urgent and most important to begin with. After cataloging the questions I collected and conducting over four hundred personal interviews, it became clear that health is the number one topic most women need to talk about with their mothers, followed by death and dying, money, and aging. These four aspects of life dramatically affect the quality of your mother's current and future life and your own, and they need to be discussed whether or not you get along with her. If this is the case for you, *My Mother, My Friend* will make it easier for you to discuss these topics.

Not as urgent, but definitely important in completing unfinished business from the past and enjoying the present, are four more topics: resolving conflict, family secrets, romance and intimacy, and self-image and beauty.

The final two topics speak to the heart and soul and help to celebrate the human and the divine in our mothers: spirituality and appreciation. Discussing your beliefs about the mysteries of life and death shape who you become and how you live. Understanding your mother's spiritual perspective can go a long way to understanding more about yourself. Taking the time to appreciate your mother strengthens the bond between you and celebrates the gifts you have given each other.

Throughout these pages, you will be guided through the process of changing your patterns of communication and, ultimately, your relationship to your mother and yourself. Through thoughtfully phrased questions, practical exercises, sample dialogues, and communication tips, you will learn how you can talk to your mother, woman to woman, about the issues of life and death and everything in between. When you develop a pattern of communicating openly, you are well on your way to forging a deeper and more rewarding relationship and preparing yourself for the changes that your mother's aging inevitably brings.

You will be asked to journal your thoughts and questions, and record your mother's answers (in written, audio, or video format). This may seem time-consuming, but you will be forever grateful that you did this. Someday in the future, you will want and need the information I'm asking you to gather. Your mind will not remember the details you need, but you will have a journal filled with critical information and some of your most precious shared memories, which you'll be able to refer back to as needed.

If you feel comfortable with your mother and just need a little direction on how to broach a particular issue, you can go directly to the chapter that interests you, read through the questions, and start from there. If you have a particular question in mind, look at the Contents page for the appropriate chapter. Then review my suggestions in the Introduction for wording a specific question and creating a comfortable setting. If you want a more organized program, consider this book a guidebook. Use it over a ten-month period, a chapter a month. After you've read the Introduction and know how to proceed, share the book with your mom. Together you can approach one chapter a month and get to know each other better at a leisurely pace, planning the activities and then asking the questions at the end of each chapter. You'll always begin the process with easy questions and work up to the more challenging, intimate ones.

By using the information in this book, you will learn how to release or change patterns that don't work in your relationship with your mother and maximize the ones that do. You will carry on your mother's legacy of love. You will discover more about yourself. You will help your mother recognize her own significance and live with more vitality and financial security. Both of you will become more physically, emotionally, intellectually, and spiritually enriched. When your mother's time comes to pass on, you will know what her wishes are and what to do. You will become stronger, gentler, and wiser. Most important, you will learn to appreciate and celebrate each other.

Be brave, count your blessings, and enjoy the questions.

Mary Mardante

Getting to Know You

How to Begin

It's been seven years since my mother passed away and I still have questions I want to ask her. Sitting at my desk, I glance at a photograph next to my computer. It's a wrinkled black and white snapshot of my mother and me, lying on our backs, sleeping peacefully in her twin bed. The year is 1953, and I am six months old. I am dressed in baby bunting, and look like a Kewpie doll with my brown hair twirled into a single curl on the top of my head. Mom is thirty-three. Her face is shiny, and her arms are folded up over her head. She's wearing a sleeveless nightie and a thin gold bracelet around her left wrist. Her painted nails shimmer, and she looks as beatific as the Madonnas she used to collect.

What memories that photo evokes.

I am fourteen years old and excited because I have just found this picture of myself and Mom that I had never seen before. I show it to her, and she reminisces about how jubilant she felt after I was born, because she'd been told she would never be able to have children.

Fast-forward ten years, to the night of my grandfather's funeral. Mom and I are rummaging through old photos, and I happen on that same lovely snapshot. Once again, I show it to her, and this time she shares some gossip.

"Mary, you know you were named after my mother. Thank goodness, though, that both grandmothers had the middle name Louise or there would have been even more competition between them than there already was." Ooh, I hadn't heard *that* before.

Now, at the age of forty-five, I am troubled by questions that never got asked, and frustrated by half-understood information that leads me up blind alleys because Mom's not here to help me make sense of it. For instance, after she died, what can I make of my father's saying, "I don't know why your mother was seeing a psychiatrist all those years." She never told Dad why she was seeing a psychiatrist! Come to think of it, I can't remember her telling me either. What was she going through? What turmoil? What was on her mind? Like most other daughters, I took for granted that I knew everything there was to know about my mother. Consequently, there is so much that I will never know.

Over the years, each time Mom and I revisited the old, white Gimbels department store dress box in which she kept our photos, fascinating pieces of information were revealed. My mother was an open book. I could ask her anything and if she knew the answer, she'd tell me. Whether we were shopping, going out to lunch, taking a walk, doing jigsaw puzzles, or, later, lying together on her hospital bed, she had a story to tell.

Mom chatted about our family history and revealed her dreams. She also told me what I should do with the rest of my life, which, of course, drove me mad. Crazy making as it was at times, I look back on our life together, now that time has softened my disappointment in her human frailty, and I realize what a gift my mother was. I see how important those question-and-answer sessions were to both of us. My questions gave her permission to be more than a mother—permission to be herself. Her answers shaped my success and, more important, my sense of self and the memories that fashion my future.

> *always the beautiful answer who asks a more*
> *beautiful question.*
> —E. E. CUMMINGS, in *Collected Poems*

How can a daughter begin relating to her mother in new ways? How can she begin to share confidences and leave behind unsuccessful ways of communicating? How can a daughter get the answers she needs to questions she is afraid to ask—or hasn't thought to ask—that will affect both her mother's current and future well-being and her own?

Two simple words will begin answering these questions: time and friendship. Let's look at *time* first, because that has the greatest impact on how you perceive your mother. You won't want to hear what I'm going to say, but as my mother used to say, "It's for your own good." One day you will no longer be able to hug your mom. One day, if you aren't close, you'll no longer be able to hope for a better relationship. You won't be able to say, "I'm sorry. Let's try again." The sooner you let this sink in, the easier it will be for you to know her better, enjoy more of what you do share, and help both of you live with more meaning and love. Buddhists believe the way to happiness is to keep death over your shoulder because it reminds you to live in the richness of the moment. This is what I think we need to do with our mothers: pin this notion of the preciousness of life on to our shoulder to keep us from withdrawing or getting distracted when things with Mom aren't going the way we planned.

The second word to keep in mind is *friendship*. Consider this idea for a moment. We form friendships for many reasons, but there is one common denominator: we choose our friends because we feel safe to be ourselves with them. Think of your best woman friend. What makes your friendship work so well? You feel free to tell her everything. She understands. You accept that she's always eight minutes late because whenever you are PMS-ing, she lets you whine about things you know you shouldn't be whining about. You ask her what she'd do. She commiserates. She tells you that you'll get through it. She brainstorms solutions with you. You laugh together. When you're sick, she brings you jelly doughnuts with your chicken soup. You talk about your mothers and how they drive you crazy and how much you still love them. She's your friend because you know you'll feel better after being with her.

Have you ever thought about your mother that way? What if it really were possible to have the same type of relationship with your mother as you do with your best friend—or even better?

True friends are those who really know you but
love you anyway.
—EDNA BUCHANAN, *Suitable for Framing*

If you are close to your mother your answer will be, "I already do," or "My mother is my best friend," or "I can't imagine life without my mother." You and she have been friends since before you can remember, or you have a clear memory of the moment you realized she was not just your mother, she was also your friend. That's great. Then use this book as a way to focus on areas of your relationship that you may not have explored yet.

If you are distanced from your mother, you may say, "My mother has never been my friend, and I specifically chose my friends because they weren't like my mother." Or you may find yourself somewhere in between—close but not friends—the way I experienced my mother—until I started writing this book and realized that one of the greatest gifts she gave to me was her friendship. If this describes you, allow yourself to try on calling your mother a friend, like I did. At first, it may feel constricting, like a pair of too-tight shoes. But carry that thought around in your head for a while, and your energy will shift. You'll begin to think of your mother differently. Your expectations will change. It will become easier to give her the love, respect, and caring you afford your dearest women friends, even when she's behaving badly or you're having a rough day. You'll be able to set limits calmly and maintain your self-respect instead of doing or saying something that makes you feel terrible and act even worse.

Friendship with your mother creates a space for you to want to know more about her. The time you spend together is easier and more interesting. You both find yourselves a little more willing to share parts of yourself you've kept hidden. And instead of feeling deep regret or guilt, you will feel a deep sense of gratitude. You'll give thanks for your mother and for the person you've become in learning how to befriend her while she is still alive.

If We Don't Really Know Our Mothers, We Can't Really Know Ourselves

Harriet Lerner, psychologist and author of *The Dance of Deception—A Guide to Authenticity and Truth-Telling in Women's Relationships*, believes that our relationship with our mother is one of the most significant and influential relationships of our lives. In her audiotape, *On Mothers and Daughters*, she eloquently defines the importance of understanding our mothers.

> *Before all else we are daughters. . . . If we don't really know our mother we can't really know ourselves . . . and if we can't recognize her competence, we can't really value and love our own self . . . and if we don't love and value ourselves, we can't really love another person as fully as each of us would be capable of loving.*

Being willing to know your mother at a deeper level is an act of courage. She will no longer be *just* your mother—the woman who is there to meet your every need—to hug you, fix your dinner, wash your clothes, or go to your volleyball games. She will become a woman in her own right, with hopes and dreams and needs and desires just like you. She will share parts of herself that you have never known about. If you prepare and welcome her into your heart as you would a dear friend, her truth will be a gift of self-discovery for both of you.

How Do I Expand My Awareness of My Mother?

If you find yourself struggling to widen your perspective of your mother, try surprising yourself out of your own patterns. One unusual and very effective technique is to call your mother by her first name on occasion. If that's too bold, then consider asking her to try an experiment with you. Ask her if you may call her by her first name a few times just to see if it expands your awareness of her as a friend. If she says no, say her first name to yourself when you think of her. This is a big step, and one you won't likely take most of the time. But for some women it can be a powerful acknowledgment of the multidimensional woman outside the narrow role of mother.

Sarah's mother was in her eighties and in poor health. She experienced her mother as a cranky woman with whom she found it very difficult to talk. One day in frustration, Sarah yelled her mother's name, "Olivia!" Startled, her mother began to cry. Overcome with guilt, Sarah called out in a soft, loving voice, "Olivia, Olivia, I love you, Olivia."

From that time on, Sarah recalls, she never looked at her mother the same way. "My mother became a person to me. She was no longer 'just' my mother. I realized that she really was separate from me and had a right to her feelings, just as I did. No matter how ill tempered she was, I was able to love her more fully after that."

Calling your mother by her first name, even if only to yourself, is only one of many strategies that begin shifting your perspective of your mother to include woman and friend. Another easy and meaningful approach is to ask her a question about what she wants or what interests her. Even if you don't get an answer immediately or, for that matter, ever, the seed has been planted, and with time and a little nurturing, you may be surprised by an unexpected flower, as was my friend Joan.

How About If You Teach Me How to Bake Bread?

Joan, a successful business consultant, author, and syndicated columnist, had a close relationship with her mother as she was growing up. But as Joan became more successful in her career, her relationship with her mother became more distant. There was less and less to say because they didn't know how to talk about the growing disparity in their lifestyles and interests.

"When I was forty, my mother stopped driving, which limited her lifestyle dramatically," Joan recalls. I whined for years to my husband about how my mother would be so much better if she'd get out, take a class, join a club—do anything so she wasn't so housebound. David finally said to me, 'Get off your mother's case. What makes you think you can live your mother's life better than she can? You don't call her. You don't spend time with her. You just whine to me about it.'

"I said, 'I'm just trying to be helpful,' but in my heart I knew he was right. I told myself, she's in her late sixties and she's not going to change, so what can I do to come halfway?"

Joan remembered that her mother had always been a wonderful baker who talked about how relaxing it was to knead dough. "So I called her one night and said, 'How about if you teach me how to bake bread?' After a good hard laugh, she retorted, 'How about buying yourself a bread machine? With your schedule, it will be a lot easier.' I told her I was serious about wanting to learn from her because she was such a good baker. She finally agreed and told me what ingredients to buy. The following Sunday I showed up at her house at ten in the morning with two bags of groceries and a notebook. For the next six hours, I sat at her feet and wrote down every move she made. At the end of the day, I had two perfect loaves under my arms and the realization that it was the most time I'd spent with my mom in ten years. We had laughed and talked more than we had when I was a kid.

"When I walked out the door with my prize, I turned around and said to her, 'Why don't we do this again.' She said, 'All right, you're on. Next time we do wheat.' Sure enough, the following Sunday I learned to do wheat. Three weeks later, I asked her to do Christmas cookies. She said, 'Joan, you know how to do cookies.' I felt like a little girl again as the words tumbled out, 'I know. But I want to do them with you.' So we made Christmas cookies together, and on Christmas Eve she showed up at my house with her cookies. I brought out mine, and we arranged them together on platters for our families. We were closer that Christmas and we've been closer ever since. I realized I wasn't just baking bread; I was baking a relationship."

Joan's efforts in thinking about her mother's interests and asking a single question, "How about teaching me how to bake bread?" saved their relationship. Her mother felt more valued by Joan, and Joan sharpened a critical skill—appreciation—that is often dulled in the competitive business world.

If you find yourself saying that you're willing to go deeper but your mother isn't, there's hope. If it's more than you can do even to be in the same room with your mother, I still encourage you to hold a space in your heart for healing and continue to think of her becoming a friend. The power of prayer and positive intention is no longer just a religious ritual. As you'll discover when you read the spirituality chapter, research has shown that asking a higher power for a positive outcome and holding that desire in a space of love literally heals people from a distance. If you remain open and willing, your relationship will shift. It may be barely noticeable at first, so pay close attention, and trust your intention and intuition.

When I started writing this book, my friend Linda said that she thought the book was a great idea, but it wouldn't work for her. When I asked why, she said that her mother, a first-generation German, didn't believe in sharing any of her own personal feelings or family memories because it's private and "no one else's business." (The German culture, Linda explained, can be very reserved and private.) Having met her mother a few times at family gatherings and finding her warm and outgoing, this was new information to me. I was surprised to learn that Linda, who is strong, assertive, emotionally sensitive, and smart, had longed for a deeper connection with her mother but hadn't been able to achieve that breakthrough. Linda explained that she had sensitively approached her mother several times, asking to know her at a more personal level, all of which led to her mother's withdrawal. Finally Linda had given up. I explained the idea of time, friendship, and positive intention (you'll learn about this in just a few pages) to her. I told her that if we visualize a positive outcome, watch for an opening, say what we need to say with love, and are persistent, miracles can happen. That was a year ago. She agreed that was true for some people, but probably not with her mother.

Four months later we talked again, and Linda said there had been no change, but she had decided to remain patiently persistent "to the end," hoping that things could change in the future. I offered to send her a first draft of the chapter on conflict, which she accepted.

I called Linda tonight—it's been six months since we last talked. She told me there was still no real change, but as I listened to her, I heard change everywhere. She said, "One day my mother, sister, and I were driving in the car recently when my mother started to share a story about her own mother. I jumped in excitedly and said one word, 'Really?' which led to my mother's turning silent. I withdrew too. Later my sister told me that the reason she had more success than I did in hearing our mother's stories was because I showed too much emotion, which made our German mother very uncomfortable. My sister said she got more stories from Mom because she learned to stay very calm and quiet when Mom was talking about personal things."

What an insight! A positive intention of "I want to know my mother and I will be patiently persistent until the end" led to a small break-through and tremendous awareness for future conversations.

Determine What You Want from Your Conversation

Why do you want to talk to your mother? What do you hope to gain by having a heart-to-heart conversation? When you know what you want to achieve, you'll be able to ask the right questions at the right time and in the right place. You may have several items you want to address, because your relationship with your mother is multidimensional. Several typical reasons for starting a mother-daughter dialogue are listed in the box below. They're not all-inclusive by any means, and I've provided them simply to get you started. Choose as many reasons as you think are relevant, and feel free to add your own.

As the relationship with your mother evolves, your ambitions and desires may change. You may discover that you've outgrown an area of concern. You may, for instance, no longer need confirmation that Mom loves you. You may want to find out information on a family member, or to learn why Mom never wants to talk about her health, or to know where she keeps her legal documents, or, hard as it is to discuss, to learn what her last wishes are.

Why Do You Want to Talk to Your Mom?

- ❑ To fill in a memory?
- ❑ To confirm your experiences?
- ❑ To talk to her about her health?
- ❑ To resolve a disagreement?
- ❑ To air a family secret?
- ❑ To gain (or earn) approval?
- ❑ To get more attention and nurturing?
- ❑ To share your spiritual beliefs?
- ❑ To relieve your guilt?
- ❑ To be forgiven?
- ❑ To take your relationship to a deeper level?
- ❑ To appreciate and celebrate her?

Turn Your Reason into an Intention

Select the one reason that seems most important to you, and write it out—for example:

- I want to *talk to my mother about her health.*
- I want to *find out the truth about my adoption.*
- I want to *know what she thinks about getting older.*

This will become your intention. Having a solid reason for beginning the journey will keep you focused and also influence the outcome. It will serve to shape your conversations and smooth any rough edges along the way. If you get stuck, return to this intention and say it out loud to yourself.

What Questions Should I Ask?

After you understand some of the reasons why you want to deepen your relationship with your mother, make a list of questions in your journal. Base your questions on the intention you decided on. Let your mind wander. Don't worry about whether she'll answer them or what you'll sound like. This is a starting point. You can worry about how to articulate your questions later.

Sample Intention and Questions

My intention: I want to talk to my mother about her health.

- Are there any medical conditions in our family history (grandparents, aunts, uncles on both sides of our family) that I'm not aware of yet?
- What concerns you most about your health?
- If you became seriously ill, how would you like me to respond?

The list is limited only by your interest, imagination, and comfort level. These are the same questions you'd want to ask a new friend—not a one-dimensional cardboard figure created by circumstance: mother. Not a perpetually frowning or rejecting parent. Whatever cliché you maintain about your mom, it's only part of the story. There's much more.

Practice Active Listening

In my work as a professional speaker and trainer in the areas of communication and stress management, I often ask, "What is one of the best ways a person can show you appreciation?" The most common response I've received from the thousands of people I've encountered is: "When a person listens to me." Following are five suggestions to help you become a better listener in conversations with your mother.

- *Suspend judgment.* At this point you're probably making lists in your mind of all the times your mother was judgmental—all the times you wanted her to have an open mind and she had to tell you what you were doing wrong. Psychologists call this *stockpiling,* and it doesn't accomplish a thing except make it harder to move forward. Throw away your list. At such times turn-around is not fair play. Suspending judgment is probably one of the hardest things you're going to have to do in your mother's presence. If you find yourself disagreeing with her or disliking what she's saying, try repeating to yourself, "Open mind, open heart," as a way to diffuse the negative thought. Visualize yourself opening up like a beautiful rose. Remember that you're an adult with discretionary power over your life. She can't keep you from eating cookies in bed or watching television past your bedtime or playing hooky from work. You asked for her opinion. She's giving it to you. Be willing to hear it. You'll find a gold mine if you can stay open.
- *Let her finish her sentences.* Interrupting shuts down communication. Let your mother finish her sentences before you speak up. You will find that if you pause just a little longer than you are usually comfortable with, you'll get more information.
- *Clarify your understanding.* Repeat back to your mother in your own words what you think she said and ask if that is what she meant: "Mom, let me make sure I'm on the same wavelength as

you. When you said that you couldn't believe how things turned out, did you mean that you were pleased with what actually happened?"

- *Acknowledge what she says.* Acknowledge your mother's feelings. This doesn't mean you are necessarily agreeing with her, simply that you understand. This is one of the most effective methods of listening, validating, and understanding a person that I have ever come across. Here are three examples:

  "It looks as if . . ." *or* "It sounds as if . . ." *or* "It seems as if . . ." [you are disappointed things turned out the way they did; you wish we were going out].

  "I'm wondering if you're feeling . . ." [annoyed that I'm late; sad that I couldn't make it].

  "I'm guessing that you . . ." [were scared about what would have happened if you hadn't been there; are excited about going to the Caribbean].

- *Ask open-ended questions.* Open-ended questions give you more than yes or no answers. They give you more detailed information—for example:

  "What happened once you knew the answer?" [Rather than, "Did you discover the answer?"]

  "What kinds of things did you do?" [Rather than, "Did you go out to dinner?"]

  "How did you come to that conclusion?" [Rather than, "Why did you do that?"]

Visualize a Positive Outcome

Lee became worried when her very active, and aging, mother suddenly stopped bowling. Lee was afraid to say anything. She was afraid her mother would explain that she was preparing to die. After changing her intention from one of worry to one of curiosity, and visualizing her mother as a healthy person, Lee finally broached the subject: "Did you quit bowling because of health problems, Mother?" Lee's mother's response was succinct: "The other team members died or had strokes. It was too hard to field a new team, so I moved on. Now I'm in a kitchen band; I play a percussion tool—a washboard." Lee was relieved and realized how important it was for her own peace of mind to shift her per-spective from worry to curiosity.

Before you begin a new chapter with your mother, get yourself in the right frame of mind so that you are physically and emotion-ally comfortable. Preparation includes relaxing and imagining a posi-tive outcome. Spend five minutes with this relaxation exercise to loosen up.

1. Find a quiet room away from distractions—a place where you feel warm and safe.
2. Sit in a comfortable position.
3. Close your eyes and relax. Count slowly from ten down to one each time you breathe in. Relax your body as you breathe out.
4. Imagine you are sitting at the kitchen table with your mother, sa-voring a batch of her freshly baked cookies or your favorite meal. You're feeling happy and safe.
5. Imagine reaching out across the table and taking your mother's hand. You look into your mother's eyes and send her unconditional love. She smiles and sends her love back to you through her eyes.
6. Notice your mother breathing in harmony with you. With each breath, you feel closer and more loving with each other.
7. Stay with this feeling of connection and love for a few minutes. Then gently bring your awareness back to the room. In your mind's ear, hear your mother thank you for your love. Thank her in return.
8. Throughout the rest of the day, allow yourself to drift back to the images, sounds, and feelings that surfaced when you and your mother sat quietly together. Bring this feeling with you the next time you sit down to talk with your mother.

Establish a Positive Direction

You want your first conversation to be as easy and nonalarming as possi-ble, opening the door only as far as it feels comfortable. You are both on a journey to get past obstacles that have been preventing you from knowing each other as whole human beings—woman to woman, friend to friend.

Recovering memories, discovering secrets, and uncovering the truth is a process, so if your intention is to ask difficult questions, work up to them. It helps to build rapport with lighter subjects, to create an atmosphere that is warm and conducive to confiding. If you expect that your mother will be resistant to your questioning and suggestions, make sure to read Conversation 5, which covers how to deal with conflict. You'll find sixteen common answers that a resistant mother might say when asked a question, followed by specific words you can respond with to keep the conversation going.

The best way to start a dialogue with your mother is to make a statement of positive direction. Positive direction is stating your intention in optimistic language.

Sample Statements of Positive Direction

- "Mom, I found this book of questions that would help us know each other better and that would be fun to do together."
- "To help us patch up that disagreement we had, I'd like to talk with you for a few minutes about what happened and figure out a better way to do it next time."
- "I really appreciate it when you tell me what's going on for you. It makes it easier for me to be honest with you."

When Is the Best Time to Begin?

Consider the optimal timing for both of you. Your timing is as individual as your relationship. There's no "right" time, and there's no "perfect" place.

Judith's relationship with her mother took a dramatic turn one night when the dishwasher died at the end of a large and elaborate Thanksgiving dinner. All through the night, as mother and daughter handwashed and dried pots, pans, dishes, glassware, and silverware, they talked and reminisced, discovering bonds each thought were severed. Sometime in the early hours of the morning, mother and daughter hugged, having reconnected in a way that had eluded them for years.

Fortuitous accidents can happen, but don't count on the dishwasher's breaking to start the ball rolling. Anticipate an occasion when you can rely on goodwill and warmth to open the communication channels. Here are some ideas—feel free to add your own.

- Birthdays
- Family reunions
- Your parents' anniversary
- During the holidays after a meal
- On a lazy afternoon with nothing much going on

Where Is the Best Place to Talk?

The best place to talk could be anywhere. But remember that in a situation when you may be feeling like Daniel in the lion's den, you'll always feel safer and more in control if you're in your own room or a space from which you can easily exit. If your mother tends to emote loudly, a private space, rather than a restaurant or café, may be preferable. If your mother needs to be outside her own home in order to open up, a walk in the park may be perfect. Choose a place to chat where both of you are relaxed and at your ease. A traffic jam or the anteroom in a dentist's office where you're waiting for root canal might not be optimal. Don't let your anxiety sabotage communication.

Just because you think getting to know your mother better is a great idea doesn't mean your mother will, so choose your time and place carefully.

Best Places to Talk with Your Mother

- Sitting on her bed
- Sitting at the kitchen table
- On the phone
- While shopping
- During the commercials while watching a TV movie
- In a letter or journal that you send to share with each other

Once you have decided on the time and place, consider how to ask your first question, and mentally rehearse how you'd like the conversation to turn out.

How Do I Create the Right Mood?

Consider your own emotional state when you're about to engage in a heart-to-heart with your mom. The week you break up with the man of yesterday's dreams, or lose your job, or get hit with a huge tax bill may not be the best time to expect yourself to be open and giving. Think about the following, and add your own ideas to the list.

- Are you and your mother more at ease with each other in the morning, at lunch, or at the end of the day?
- Are you rested and relaxed? Or have you just come through a crisis?
- Is there something going on in your life that you need to resolve on your own before you talk with your mother?

What's the Best Way to Record Her Answers?

You have several options. The important thing is to do it. One of the nicest mementos I have of my mother is her voice on audiotape. I wish I had videotaped her too. Until your mother is no longer with you, you have no idea how precious the sound of her voice is, especially when she says, "I love you."

Here are several options that work well.

- Write a letter to your mother, and ask her to write back.
- Give her a gift of stationery, and include your first letter in the box.
- Buy or borrow a hand-held audiocassette recorder, and tape your questions. Give your mom the recorder, show her how to use it, and ask her to record her answers at her leisure. Do this for each question or session. You'll be able to keep more than your memory of her.
- Videotape her. But realize that being taped makes some people self-conscious.

- Talk in person. Take notes while she's talking, or record your thoughts in your journal within an hour after you've been together.
- As you talk on the phone, record her voice on your answering machine. Use a different tape from the one you ordinarily use for your machine, and remember to change it.

The Chinese have a saying: "The journey of a thousand miles begins with a single step." You've taken that crucial first step by planning how best to approach your mother. Congratulations! Many people fail in their communications because they never think about what results they want, how to say what they want to say, or what the other person may need in order to give you the results they want. You have. Celebrate!

> *As long as one keeps searching, the answers come.*
> —JOAN BAEZ (interview)

Activities to Do with Your Mom

To create rapport before you begin your question—asking or while you're asking questions, consider the following activities.

- ❑ Go out for a special lunch once a month.
- ❑ Cook or bake together.
- ❑ Ask your mother to include you in an activity she and her friends normally do together.
- ❑ Invite your mother to participate in an activity with you and your friends.
- ❑ Have a mother-daughter brunch with your friends and your mother's friends.
- ❑ See a therapist together.
- ❑ Take a vacation together.
- ❑ Watch a video together about mother-daughter relationships:
  - *Beloved.* A slave is visited by her deceased daughter's spirit.
  - *Eating.* A realistic look at the role food plays in women's lives, including a sixtyish mother at her daughter's fortieth birthday party.

- *Home for the Holidays.* A humorous and touching story about a thirtyish daughter who goes home to her parents' home for Thanksgiving.
- *The Joy Luck Club.* Through flashbacks, four Asian women learn more about their mothers' pasts and themselves.
- *One True Thing.* A thirtyish daughter returns home to care for her mother who has been diagnosed with cancer.
- *Postcards from the Edge.* An actress who lived in her actress mother's shadow is forced to move back in with her mother and learns to change her life.
- *Sense and Sensibility.* A mother and her three daughters in the late eighteenth century lose their inheritance and look for men to marry.
- *Terms of Endearment.* A tearjerker that shows the love and differences between a mother and daughter in their day-to-day lives.

Questions to Ask Yourself

- Why do I want to talk with my mother?
- What is my intention in talking with Mom?
- What questions do I want to ask her?
- When is the best time to talk?
- Where is the best time to talk?
- How will I create the right mood?
- How will I record her answers?
- What listening techniques will most help me keep communication open?

I Am Woman

Health and Sexuality

I was nineteen in 1972, and one of those young women who wanted to experience the pill. Actually, it wasn't the pill I wanted; what I wanted was what the pill allowed me to experience. AIDS was not a concern back then (AYDS was the diet candy my mother ate to control her weight), so my only concern was not getting pregnant with my husband-to-be. I can still remember making a nervous phone call to an OB/GYN who was recommended by my sophisticated college friend, Colleen. She promised he would prescribe birth control pills without asking if I were married and a legal adult (age twenty-one in Wisconsin). I was told to request a Pap smear and then casually request birth control pills before I left.

When I arrived, I avoided eye contact with other women as I paced in the small waiting room and felt my body shiver as I walked into the exam room and saw the stirrups awaiting me for the first time. After looking up at the ceiling for what seemed like forever, my first gynecological checkup was finally over. I took a deep breath, cleared my throat, asked the question exactly as coached, and walked out with three months' worth of sample birth control pills and a prescription for another year. Overcome with relief, I celebrated my success and never, ever thought about telling my mother.

What about you? What were your first experiences of becoming a sexually mature woman? Was there a defining moment? Was it the first time you menstruated? First time you wore a bra? First time you went to the doctor for a "female" checkup? First time you experienced sex? Did you tell your mother? What did she say? Write a paragraph or two on what you remember about growing into a woman. The next time you're with your mother, ask her the same question. Not only will you find some interesting, touching, and maybe even humorous stories, but your dialogue will also prepare you for a discussion of current health issues that you and your mother will want to be aware of.

Why Should I Talk with My Mother About Her Health?

The top three killers of women are heart disease, lung cancer, and breast cancer, with more women dying each year from heart disease than all cancers, accidents, and diabetes combined. Depression, osteoporosis, ovarian cancer, cervical cancer, alcoholism, and obesity also plague women in astonishing numbers. And if that isn't enough to make us want to talk to our mothers about health issues, consider this: at least 80 percent of all heart attacks and cancers occur in people over the age of fifty-five.

What concerns me most about these statistics is that so many women know about the risks but live in denial, thinking health problems happen to other people, not them or their families. Or they worry obsessively in private, but don't check out their body's messages. They ignore warning signs until their illness has progressed to a crisis stage. I am not exaggerating when I say that in every single one of the hundreds of stress management seminars I've done over the years, at least one woman tells a story—without my prompting—of how she ignored early warning signs that led to her cancer or heart disease. What amazes me even more is that many of the women in the room are nodding in agreement with her but are not able, for whatever reason, to heed that call in their own lives.

> *Thousands upon thousands of persons have studied disease.*
> *Almost no one has studied health.*
> —ADELLE DAVIS, *Let's Eat Right to Keep Fit*

Finding a way through the medical maze requires information, awareness, and assertiveness. If your mother doesn't understand how to navigate the medical system, I urge you to become her advocate—not just for her sake, but also because it will better prepare you if the time comes for you to confront the system yourself. Trust me on this: I've been there. Working women's health care costs are 45 percent higher than men's, and knowing how to keep your own costs down, yet still get the care you need, in many cases requires a heavy dose of assertiveness and research.

It's a different world today from the one in which our mothers were born. We've learned that a long life doesn't always go hand in hand with a healthy life, and what a woman does in her twenties through her fifties is shaping the health she will have in her sixties, seventies, and eighties. We are part of the movement that is creating a cognitive shift in our culture from thoughts of illness and treatment to health and prevention. Let's use this knowledge to help our mothers live healthier lives for as long as they are with us.

Of all the conversations you can have with your mother, health is one of the most important. Your life and your mother's may depend on it. In my seminars, so many women tell me how they wished they'd had this information for many reasons:

- Their mother had died, and these daughters no longer had access to their medical history to clarify their own health challenges.
- Conversations about their mother's health could have saved their mothers a lot of needless suffering, and in some cases, an untimely death.
- When their mothers got sick, the daughters had been forced to respond in crisis mode rather than prevention mode.
- Many daughters hadn't known how to deal with a sudden accident or illness that required them to be caregivers to their mothers.

Things Are Not Always What They Seem

A month after my mother died, I was at a cousin's wedding and sat down to talk with my mother's three sisters. I asked them to tell me about the family's health history. One of my aunts said, "Well, you know your grandmother died of colon cancer."

"Colon cancer? Since when?" I said incredulously. "I thought Mom said she died of breast cancer."

My mind raced as I recalled the last conversation I could remember having with my mother about my grandmother's death. I was seventeen. What did I miss in the translation? Suddenly I was overwhelmed with memories. My father had had a malignant tumor removed from the outside of his colon ten years earlier, and his mother had died from colon cancer. I also knew that there is a strong connection between ovarian cancer, which my mother died from, and colon cancer. I saw my life and my colon flash in front of me. Two words immediately took on new meaning: *fiber* and *colonoscopy.*

I'm lucky that my mother's three sisters are still alive and can fill in some of the blanks for me, but there are still important questions I'll never know the answer to because Mom's no longer here, such as, "What caused your depression?" "What was it like for you to have a hysterectomy?" "What was menopause like?" It's not that I couldn't have asked these questions while she was alive; I just never thought about it. And like so many other women, I sometimes wonder what might have happened if I'd had more health information and questions to share with my mother even a few years earlier. Be brave about talking with your mother about her health. It could save both of your lives.

> *If we are to take care of ourselves, and teach our daughters
> and their daughters how to do the same, we must know how to
> access the health-care system, how to talk to doctors, and how
> to demand respect and appropriate treatment from a system
> that is not always kind to women.*
>
> —DR. NANCY SNYDERMAN,
> *Dr. Nancy Snyderman's Guide to
> Good Health: For Women over Forty*

The women of our mothers' generation have not had access to the assertive communication courses and books that we have. They were taught to keep their personal matters, especially their health, to themselves. Inquiring about the details of another person's health was considered rude and intrusive. Women were taught to turn their care over to their physician and "follow doctor's orders." Although some of this thinking still exists, it is counteracted with the strong presence of female physicians, therapists, writers, and politicians. These women are working diligently to promote a stronger awareness of women's health issues: Dr. Nancy Snyderman, who pioneered health care tips on television news shows, Dr. Christiane Northrup, an OB/GYN physician, and Joan Borysenko, a medical researcher and healer, who made the mind-body connection a household word in women's health; Carolyn Myss, a medical intuitive, whose work has changed how we view energy and the body; Gail Sheehy, who wrote *The Silent Passage*, the definitive book on menopause; and former Texas governor Anne Richards, who crusades for women's rights and self-awareness.

If your mother is conscientious about her health, then your main goal will be to review your family health history—physical, emotional, and mental. If your mother lacks a healthy awareness of her body, if she is ill, or if you have not talked about her health with her, creating a family health tree together is a good starting point for discussing her health.

Once you have a good idea of your family's health history, you'll be better equipped to talk with her about things she can do to take better care of herself. Consider starting a walking routine, cooking a weekly low-fat meal together, or participating in some shared activity that acknowledges healthier choices.

Create a Family Health Tree

At least 3,000 of the 10,000 diseases known to medicine have a genetic component. Studies have found genetic links to many types of cancer, heart disease, diabetes, depression, Tay-Sachs disease, Alzheimer's disease, and multiple sclerosis. Afflictions such as alcoholism and even obesity can be inherited. By going back a few generations, you can uncover recessive genes that have been handed down through generations while bypassing the carrier of the gene. For example, if your father's mother had breast or uterine cancer and your father is a carrier, he can pass those genes on to you.

When you sit down with your mother to discuss your family history, take your journal with you and record her memories. Corroborate her feedback with other family members to make sure that your information is correct. If you've filled out an insurance form or a complete medical history at your doctor's office, you'll most likely already have most of the information for your immediate family, but make sure to include the health history for your parents' siblings, as well as both sets of grandparents.

> *An individual doesn't get cancer, a family does.*
> —TERRY TEMPEST WILLIAMS, *Refuge*

Carol Krause, author of *How Healthy Is Your Family Tree?* is a public affairs specialist who became interested in her family's health history when her mother and sister died from cancer. After interviewing family members and investigating death certificates, she found that more than a dozen family members had died from some type of cancer. Carol chose to have a preventative hysterectomy because of the history of ovarian cancer in her family and was also successfully treated for colon and breast cancer. She says, "There's a lot of denial out there. When I speak to groups and ask, 'How many of you know what all four of your grandparents died of?' they don't know."

Like Carol Krause, I became more concerned about my own health when my mother became ill. After her death, I began researching my family's health history, including listing all the major problems my mother had throughout her life, an exercise I will ask you to do with your own mother. The first time I made a list of her ailments, I was overwhelmed by how poor her health had been throughout her life. It was also hard to ignore the fact that I also experienced the same debilitating headaches and reproductive problems as my mother. Difficult as it was to face up to at the time, I'm so glad I did; it saved my life. Five years after Mom died, I went in to the doctor for abdominal pain and my annual pap and came out with fibroids, an ovarian cyst, and the real shock: cervical adenocarcinoma in situ (cancer in place). Shortly thereafter I had a hysterectomy and oophorectomy (ovaries removed) and reclaimed my health.

Go to your journal and at the top of a blank left-sided page, start a health history chart for yourself. On the right-hand side, make a chart for your mother. Identify any major physical injuries, illnesses, and diseases both of you have had, and group them by decade to provide you with as much detailed information as possible. (See the box for my page.) Look for patterns. You may find that you have injuries as well as diseases at similar ages, which can be helpful information for your future. On the following pages, create a health history for other family members. In addition to listing any illness, accident, or disease, include medications. For some women, this is critical information to have, for example, daughters whose mothers were treated with DES (diethylstilbestrol), widely prescribed to prevent miscarriage for more than twenty years, until it was banned in 1971. Many of these daughters were diagnosed with reproductive cancer in their twenties and thirties. Recent research is showing that *their* daughters are also showing a higher incidence of reproductive cancer at the same age.

Me and Mom—A Health History

Age	Me	Mom
Birth–10	Swallowed lye, burned throat, age 1	3 surgeries for eye problems throughout childhood
10–20		Exploratory eye surgery—age 18
20–30	Panic attacks (late 20s)	Anxiety, panic attacks. Migraine headaches (continued until death); treated with Fiorinal

Me and Mom—A Health History (continued)

Age	Me	Mom
30–40	Tension headaches (continued in 40s)	Clinical depression; anxiety treated with Valium; insomnia treated with Doriden through the remainder of her life
40–50	Fibroids, ovarian cysts Hysterectomy: cervical adenocarcinoma in situ; oophorectomy (ovaries)	Fibroid tumors, excessive bleeding, hysterectomy— age 40, large weight gain
50–60		Ear surgery to correct a genetic hearing loss, two hearing aids—age 50; Depression returns when youngest daughter leaves for college—age 58;
60–70		Falls and injures back—age 65; Degenerating disks— age 66; Spinal surgery; Ulcer that included a transfusion of tainted blood that put her in a coma for three days—age 67; "Silent killer," ovarian cancer diagnosed—dies age 70

Depression Isn't Normal

I grew up thinking that my mother's illnesses were a normal part of our family's life, yet still something that no one spoke about openly. I once overheard my father call my mother a hypochondriac, and although I was too young to know what it meant, I knew from the sound of his voice that it wasn't a good thing and promised myself I would never be like my mother. It wasn't until I took my first college psychology class that I realized that my mother was clinically depressed and that depression *wasn't* normal. And only in recent years did I discover that I was equally at risk for the disease because of my mother's history.

During my mid-twenties, before I came to realize that my marriage needed to end, I experienced anxiety attacks while driving and when I was around my friends' new babies. I snuck off to an internist who knew my parents and secretly explained my fears. "I don't feel physically ill," I said, "but more and more often I get this panicky feeling in my heart and stomach, like my mother." His response stunned me: "Stop seeing your mother for a month, take these pills, and you'll be fine." "These pills" turned out to be an antianxiety drug called Librium. I flashed back to my memory of a shoebox filled with pill containers that my mother kept in her closet on a shelf too tall for me to reach when I was young.

Not knowing what else to do and never considering telling my mother, I filled the prescription like a good girl, but couldn't bring myself to take the pills. They sat in the medicine cabinet for a week, while I felt my panic grow. In an anxious moment, I took one pill. An hour later, feeling no different and sure that if I looked in the mirror I'd see my mother's face, I frantically flushed the remaining pills down the toilet and prayed for a miracle. Not willing to tell my mother what happened, I avoided her phone calls as much as I could.

The panic continued off and on for months until one early morning I told my husband, "If you leave me alone today, I'm afraid I'll commit suicide." Shocked, my husband said he would call the hospital where he worked to see what to do. After arranging an appointment with a psychiatrist, he said he had to go to work and would come home to pick me up and take me to my appointment in the afternoon. I called my father and told him I was having a really rough time and was afraid to be alone. He said he'd be right over. I asked him not to bring my mom, but when he showed up, she was right behind him. I asked to talk to my father alone for a few minutes and began to sob, telling him I was afraid I was becoming "just like Mom." He looked at me defiantly and yelled through his whisper, "You will *never* be like your mother. None of you kids will be. Don't you *ever* think that again. Your mother is different. She can't help herself. You can." I saw tears in his eyes as he turned and walked out of the room. My mother came in and sat on the bed, patting my hand and telling me that everything would be just fine. If she heard my father's words, she never let on, and she continued to comfort me. I sat there numb, wondering what would happen to me.

> *Sadness is more like a head cold—with patience it passes.*
> *Depression is like cancer.*
> —BARBARA KINGSOLVER, *The Bean Trees*

Three hours later I was sitting in the psychiatrist's office, still wondering what would happen to me. At the end of our hour he said, "Honey, there's nothing wrong with you that a little talking wouldn't help. You don't need me. You need a therapist." I was so relieved. I was ushered into another room where I met with a nurse therapist who listened to me cry my heart out and asked that I return for a second session. At the second session, the therapist divulged (with permission) that she had also been working with my mother. What a shock! What a relief! I felt as if fireworks were exploding in my body, celebrating these new thoughts in my mind, "This therapist really understands my life and my challenges. This is *so* affirming and freeing. I can breathe again." I drove over to my mother's house right after the appointment and shared my secrets, describing my unhappiness in my marriage, my fear of having children, my concern about her health and her relationship with my father. We both cried at how scary this whole experience of anxiety and depression was and how much pressure there was to hide feelings of fear and failure from others.

I had reached another turning point in my life. I learned that avoiding my mother was not the answer for me, and the more open I was with her about my concerns—about both her and myself—the easier it was to control my anxiety. This experience marked the be-

ginning of my commitment to more self-disclosure in all of my relationships. It has been extremely uncomfortable at times but ultimately
freeing.

As you begin this journey into sensitive issues, there will be times
when you will want to pull back as I did and avoid the tough stuff (if
you haven't already). There will be times when you think that you cannot possibly relate to your mother's situation, nor she to yours. I urge
you to push through that part of you that resists doing what you know
is good for you—to be straight with yourself and to talk honestly with
your mother. Communication, whether it's with yourself or your
mother, is truly healing.

> *The World Health Organization ranks depression as the*
> *world's fourth most devastating illness. By 2020, it will have*
> *climbed to second place, exceeded only by heart disease.*
> —Reported in *The New Republic*,
> December 29, 1997

If you suspect depression in your mother, knowing how to talk with
her about it is critical to her health. Depression is an isolating disease
that affects 20 percent of the population over age sixty-five, according
to Dr. Barry Liebowitz, chief of the Mental Disorders Among the Aging
Research Branch at the National Institute of Mental Health. The National Institute of Mental Health points out that depressed people
often don't recognize their own depression, thereby forgoing helpful
treatment. Untreated, depression can lead to an increased risk of heart
disease, stroke, cancer, and osteoporosis.

Mom, Do You Think You Might Be Depressed?

There are different types and levels of severity of depression, which are
helpful to distinguish in relationship to your mother. There is the ordi-
nary symptom of feeling "down," which is normal when you've experi-

enced a loss (this is also referred to as mild depression); it responds to support. If mild depression continues and affects functioning at home and work, it is called moderate depression. Once depression becomes severe, it is considered an illness and is often associated with suicidal thoughts. Other recognized types of depression are unipolar (repeated episodes) and bipolar (alternating periods of depression and mania), as well as dysthymia (milder but similar symptoms to severe depression), psychotic depression (delusions or hallucinations), and specific syndromes such as postpartum depression (following childbirth) and SAD (seasonal affective disorder due to lack of sunlight). Depressive symptoms include: change in sleep, eating, concentration, and memory; suicidal thoughts; a lack of pleasure; increased fatigue; and at times feelings of worthlessness and guilt.

If your mother exhibits a combination of these symptoms, gather up your courage and talk with her. Find a quiet, relaxed time when the two of you are alone (so you can see her reaction and respond supportively) to ask gently, "Mom, do you think you might be depressed?" Simple as that question sounds and as difficult as it might be to say to her, or for her to hear, asking the question can act as a wake-up call. If she says no, your response is a caring, "Just checking. You've mentioned a few of the symptoms that I've read cause depression." This reply may open the door for her to talk more openly. If your mother says yes (or if she says no, but you sense otherwise), suggest she see her doctor and ask her or him to give her the Beck Depression Inventory, an uncomplicated twenty-one-item questionnaire, which has been tested for validity and reliability and is very successful in alerting a physician to potential depression.

If you sense that depression is not a factor in your mother's health, I still suggest you ask her if she ever felt depressed in her life. Some women may not be comfortable talking about depression as a clinical diagnosis, but they have felt depressed, particularly in the case of postpartum depression or after the loss of a spouse or other loved one. Talking about those feelings may create a feeling of vulnerability in your mother, but with your loving support and interest, this conversation can help you shed light on vague memories or lead you into a discussion about the connection between depression and other diseases for which she could be at risk.

Researchers at Johns Hopkins University recently completed a study on 6,000 patients with high blood pressure. Those who were also diagnosed with depression were twice as likely within the next five years to have had a heart attack as those who were not depressed. If you chose to mention this study to your mother as a fact you found startling, you could then introduce a few questions about whether depression and heart disease have ever been found in your family.

Talking About Heart Disease Symptoms

Many women are aware that heart disease is the number one killer of both men and women and kills ten times more women than breast cancer. What women tend to miss are the behaviors and symptoms in their own lives that lead to a heart attack. Thirty-five percent of adult women in this country are overweight, 24.8 percent smoke, and 62 percent don't exercise regularly, all of which contribute to heart disease. Symptoms of a heart attack are often mistaken for the flu or the normal aches and pains of aging: nausea, a feeling of congestion across the entire chest, body aches (as opposed to a shooting pain down the left arm for many men), extreme fatigue, dizziness, and ankle swelling. Talking with your mother about the symptoms of a heart attack could save your mother's life, as it did in the case of Penny's mother, Alice.

Penny, a medical records technician at a hospital, overheard a conversation by two nurses about an elderly woman who had been admitted for a heart attack. The sick woman said she had no idea that the persistent nausea she had felt the entire day before was the beginning of a heart attack. It wasn't until she couldn't catch her breath as she walked from the bed to the bathroom and started feeling dizzy that she knew something was wrong and called 911. An alarm bell went off in Penny's mind. Her mother, a healthy but sedentary woman in her seventies, had been complaining recently of a shortness of breath whenever she walked back up the basement steps of their single-story home. She anxiously called her mother that night and mentioned what she had heard. Her mother dismissed the idea of a heart attack, saying she wasn't overweight and didn't smoke. Penny began to cry, telling her mother how horrible she'd feel if something happened to her, and begged her mother to call her doctor and get her symptoms checked out. Annoyed, but also touched by Penny's obvious concern, Alice called the doctor the next morning, explained her symptoms, and was told to come to the clinic immediately. Several tests were ordered, which led to Alice's being diagnosed with angina (chest pain that can be a precursor to a heart attack). She was treated with medication and today remains symptom free. Had she waited, the doctor told her, a heart attack was imminent. Thanks to her daughter's sensitivity and willingness to discuss a touchy subject, Alice is back to playing golf and enjoying her grandchildren.

Four Life-Saving Strategies to Save Your Mother from a Heart Attack

When Penny shared her story with me, we talked about what she could do in the future should her mother actually have a heart attack. Based on my own experience of being unprepared when an elderly shopper fell into my arms in a department store one Thanksgiving weekend, I suggest four things.

- Take a CPR course if you haven't already. If you have, renew your certification.
- Carry a cell phone.
- Stay calm, breathe, and call 911.
- Ask your mother to give you her doctors' names and numbers, and carry them in your wallet, so you can call and alert them in an emergency.

Go to the Doctor with Your Mother

Penny can also better protect her mother and herself by going with her mother to her next doctor's appointment. Lenore Howe, editor of *wellnessweb.com*, an on-line health care information provider, suggests that daughters and mothers go along to each other's doctors' appointments and take notes. Whether your mother is health savvy or not, often it is difficult to remember all the things you want to cover or what a doctor tells you, and having someone else there can be reassuring and helpful.

If your mother is reserved, quiet, or even passive, have her write down her questions before the appointment, and then make sure they are asked while she is there. Because many women still treat a physician as an authority figure, they are reluctant to speak up, and in the midst of illness or pain, they may forget the question and the answer. Howe reminds women that doctors depend on women's input and that we need to remind ourselves that physicians are hired help. "They may be expensive hired help," Howe explains, "but they are being paid to take care of us."

Know How to Access Your Mother's Health Records

As important as asking the right questions of your doctor is knowing how to access medical records for your mother or yourself. With the number of specialty physicians, referrals, and insurance billing mistakes dramatically increasing, you want to check these records periodically. Jane Sarasohn-Kahn, a health care economist and consultant, says that access to medical records is different from state to state and from doctor to doctor. To secure your mother's records for her, the place to start is with her primary care physician. Any specialists that your mother sees should send their records to the primary doctor; however, Sarasohn-Kahn points out, this exchange is too often overlooked. If you want to access your mother's records for her, she must write and sign a letter explicitly giving you permission to access the records. Make two copies of this letter: one for yourself and one for her safe deposit box (make sure you are a joint signer on her box). Even better, ask your mother to have her attorney include the permission in her will. Some medical practitioners have different ideas about what constitutes a medical record, so be prepared for surprises and the potential need to retain an attorney if the records are denied.

From Hot Flashes to Power Surges

Gail Sheehy, in *The Silent Passage*, cites a study done by Professor Phyllis Mansfield that found that mothers are third in line when a woman wants information about menopause. Five hundred women were surveyed and said that they sought out a friend first, books second, their mother third, and their doctor last.

Almost 4,000 women become menopausal every day in the United States, and over 40 million women will pass through menopause in the next twenty years, according to the North American Menopause Society (NAMS). NAMS reminds women that menopause is a natural event, not a disease, with physical as well as psychosocial changes accompanying midlife that can contribute to serious health problems such as heart disease, breast cancer, and osteoporosis.

Stacy was mystified by her inability to conceive. When she was thirty-five, she finally went through a battery of tests and was shocked to find out she was going through early menopause. When she told her mother, Ruth, about it, her mother responded matter-of-factly, "Oh yes, all the women in our family did. Your sister started at twenty-seven." Stacy was stunned that neither her mother nor her sister had thought to tell her this vital piece of information. When she asked her mother, "Why didn't you tell me this before?" Ruth, clearly baffled, said, "I thought we had all talked about this." Stacy's sister agreed. Fighting back tears, Stacy said she had no memory of being told and asked her mother what other health mysteries existed in the family. The conversation led to a meeting with Stacy's mother, sister, and grandmother to talk about their health history.

Judy had a very different experience with her mother—one that we all hope for. When Judy felt her first hot flashes, she apprehensively went to her mother, Lois, and asked, "When did you first experience signs of menopause?" Lois, in her early seventies and still volunteering at her local church, laughed and said, "It was the year I turned fifty! I woke up one night craving chocolate, which I'd given up for Lent, and realized I was sopping wet. I thought it was withdrawal from lack of chocolate, but when I went to my doctor, he said it was the beginning of menopause." Just like a small child who falls and then looks to her mother before she decides whether to laugh or cry, Judy heard her mother's laugh and mirrored it. She told Lois she felt relieved to hear it wasn't difficult for her and that she appreciated her mother's openness in discussing such a personal subject.

> *Honey, those aren't hot flashes! Those are power surges!*
> —Very wise anonymous woman

As our mothers entered these postmenopausal years, their personalities became more defined and they became more settled in their ways. This can cause us to feel that a discussion on any topic of importance is not worth the effort because, as one daughter said, "It will probably lead nowhere." Instead of giving up, I'm going to encourage you to think differently, especially when it comes to sensitive health issues: talk to your mother not about what she's doing wrong but about making healthier choices.

Helping Your Mother Make Healthier Choices

One of the most sensitive health issues to discuss with women, which contributes to heart disease and most types of cancer, is the issue of weight. Yes, we talk about our diets and how much weight we've gained, or how much weight we need to lose, but it is a brave person who confronts a woman about her need to do something about her weight. Some weight issues are connected to genetic predisposition, others to lack of exercise or poor eating habits. If you have attempted to talk to your mother about her weight and have met with resistance, look at the way you're approaching her, and ask yourself, "Is there a better way to do this?"

Jane, an avid exerciser and self-professed health nut, is a three-hour plane ride from her mother, Kay, who is retired, in her mid-seventies, and living with her second husband. Both Kay and her husband are in poor health. Jane made a conscious decision after watching her mother suffer from high blood pressure that she would do whatever it took to keep herself healthy and help her mother get healthier. Kay knows she should lose weight and exercise, but doesn't have the interest or energy to do much about it, nor does she get support from her husband. Jane lost count of the times she told her mother she needed to be more vigilant about her health and was almost ready to give up.

> *It is now recognized that 60 percent of women's cancers and 40 percent of men's cancers are nutritionally related.*
> —EBERHARD KRONHAUSEN, ED.D.,
> AND PHYLLIS KRONHAUSEN, ED.D.,
> *Formula for Life*

After Jane and I talked about how she was approaching her mother, Jane realized that she had been too focused on telling her mother to change instead of supporting and encouraging her when she did take small steps to improve her situation. When Kay mentioned during a telephone call with Jane that she'd seen a talk show discussing healthy eating for seniors, Jane recognized Kay's interest. Over the next few months, Jane found several magazine articles relating to healthy eating and copied them, and every few weeks she sent an article to her mother. Jane also included a simple recipe from her favorite cookbook, with a note saying how much her mother would enjoy preparing the recipe. When they talked, about every two weeks, Jane would ask her mother if she'd had a chance to fix the recipe she sent. Her mother often said no, which was disappointing to Jane, but she didn't give up. On her next visit to see her mother a few months later, Jane brought along the classic book, *Let's Get Well*, by Adelle Davis, as a gift. She gave the book to her mother and said with excitement, "Mom, you're going to love this book. Why don't you skim through it while I'm here and choose three recipes that appeal to you, and we can cook them together."

Jane's mother was surprised at how good the results tasted. She added that she felt less bloated and tired after she ate, and was looking forward to making the recipes again. Then Jane and Kay began to talk about food habits, their favorite comfort foods, and how to fuel the body to make it work better. Much of Kay's response had to do with the new way Jane approached her mother by continually reinforcing her ideas without being overbearing. Here are a few suggestions to help you talk with your mother about her health:

- Watch for signs of interest. Listen to what she's complaining about or what she mentions is interesting to her, and build from there. Jane heard her mother mention a talk show and used that way to begin talking about healthier foods.
- Introduce one idea or subject at a time, and build slowly. Jane introduced a few short articles with one recipe every few weeks so that her mother wasn't overwhelmed and had a chance to absorb the information, before she introduced an entire book.
- Use enthusiasm in your voice when you suggest ideas. This is important. People are much more likely to try something new when you are excited about what you're asking them to do.
- Don't give up if your mother resists. Take a deep breath, relax, and start the process over. The brain needs eight to sixteen repetitions to learn something new, so repeat, repeat, repeat.

If Your Mother Is Dealing with a Chronic Illness

There are stages of conversation when talking about chronic illness just as there are stages to a disease itself. If your mother is chronically ill, there is no question that talking about health concerns can be extremely challenging. All the uncomfortable feelings of fear, anger, sadness, disappointment, resentment, and guilt seem to show up in the oddest ways at the most inopportune times. When I found myself in this situation with my mother, my way of responding to these feelings was to face the truth head-on with her. There were times that she wept as we talked, and I encouraged it, and there were times I felt myself breaking and allowed the tears to come. What I found is that my mother looked to me to help her cope, and the more open I was, the easier it was for her to respond bravely to her challenges. This in turn inspired me to continue encouraging her, while also remaining honest.

Your listening skills will be more important than ever before in responding to your mother's illness. More than anything else, though, she'll be looking for confirmation that you're not going to abandon her. It is a strange role reversal children experience when their parents become chronically ill at an advanced age: parent becomes child, and child becomes parent. What we're aiming for here is a balance of parental nurturing and caring friendship.

Helping Your Mother Stay Healthy Is a Gift of Love

As your mother ages, your conversations with her about health may change, but the desired result is still the same: to provide information and support so that your time together is rich and fulfilling for both of you. Following are suggestions for maintaining a healthy lifestyle, along with the supportive research that will provide you with several topics of conversation:

- Be part of a loving community. If your mother is sedentary or lives alone, getting out with others will help her stay healthier. A study done by Dr L. F. Berkman with 7,000 people in Alameda County, California, found that close social ties dramatically lower disease and premature death when compared to isolated living. Breast cancer survivors in a Stanford University study who participated in weekly support groups lived on average twice as long as those who didn't participate in the support groups.
- Move your body at least thirty minutes a day. The bones and heart become stronger. Independent research done by Harvard University and the Nurses Study (an ongoing program with 84,000 nurses) found that a thirty-minute walk reduced risk of heart disease by 40 percent. Exercise also has a beneficial impact in changing eating patterns, according to a study done at Baylor University.

- Weight-train two times a week. Yes, weight-train. Miriam Nelson, Ph.D., author of *Strong Women Stay Young* and *Strong Women Stay Slim*, proved that twenty minutes twice a week of simple weight training in postmenopausal women, even sedentary women as old as ninety, builds stronger bodies and helps women live more youthful lives.

- Lower your overall fat intake, and choose "good fat" over "bad fat." Switching from saturated and trans fat to monounsaturated fat (canola, flax, and hemp oils instead of butter) lowers total cholesterol without lowering HDL. The May 1998 *Pritikin Perspective* reports: "In population studies in the Mediterranean where olive oil is used instead of butter and animal fat, heart disease rates are lower than that of the U.S." If you have to have your cheese danish, eat half, and share the rest.

- Drink 64 ounces of water (eight 8-ounce glasses) a day to flush the colon and kidneys and keep the body and brain lubricated. If you're thirsty, you're already dehydrated. Two early signs you're not drinking enough water are fatigue and lack of concentration.

- If you smoke, quit. Smoking not only increases the possibility of lung cancer, but also leeches nutrients out of the bones, leading to osteoporosis, and narrows the blood vessels, upping the risk of heart disease. According to the American Heart Association, quitting smoking is the most important thing you can do to prevent heart disease.

- Get an annual checkup that includes a mammogram, bone density test, and breast, pelvic, and rectal exams. Do a monthly breast exam. Dr. Nancy Snyderman schedules all her annual health screenings the week of her birthday.

- Keep a list of all medications you've taken and are taking, including dates and reasons for taking them. It's easy to forget the names and dosages should you encounter a crisis and need to recall them in a hospital emergency room.

- Think humorous, loving, and grateful thoughts. Loma Linda University found that fake laughter is just as effective as real laughter in reducing stress. The HeartMath Institute determined that positive emotions such as appreciation, compassion, and happiness change patterns of activity in the nervous system, reduce the production of the stress hormone cortisol, and calm the heart. Listen for your own laughter three times today. If you haven't heard it by the time you go to bed, sit up in bed and laugh out loud for ten seconds. You'll surprise yourself, and when you wake up the next day, you'll have a smile on your face. Then tell your mother to try it.

Unlock the Past and Move Toward Health

Dr. Christiane Northrup, a gynecologist and pioneer in the mind-body health movement, writes in her book, *Women's Bodies, Women's Wisdom*, that by exploring your health history you can find clues to how you are contributing to your conditions. She believes that by uncovering the patterns of illness in your family, you unlock the past that is stored in the cellular memory of your body. If your family has a history of illness, becoming more aware of the underlying issues that were present before and during the illness can help you redirect your energy. This premise originates with the belief that recognition is the first step toward making change. Regardless of our age, we have the ability to create better health, beginning with our thinking, which directs our feelings and choices and ultimately influences the quality of our life.

One of the most significant insights I had after completing my mother's health history was the pervasive theme throughout her life that illness was the status quo, punctuated with moments of health. As I began to uncover how deeply rooted this belief has been in my own mind, I was able to see how important it is to work every day at changing these messages. Some of my favorite methods are music therapy, guided imagery, intuitive meditations, and verbal affirmations while I'm walking or swimming laps. Movement and positive suggestion used at the same time strengthen resolve. I also use affirmations such as, "I choose to be healthy. I choose to nourish my body," when I'm getting ready to forgo the gym or eat something I shouldn't. Affirmations are a powerful step in changing long-standing negative patterns, *and* they are only the beginning. Taking action is the final ingredient that will bring you and your mother better health. Before you talk with your mother, ask yourself these questions and write the answers in your journal:

- What are my beliefs about my health?
- How has my mother influenced my beliefs about health?
- If I were in control of my mother's health (which I'm not), I'd want her to . . .
- What I most need to do to maintain better health is . . .

When You Have Your Health, You Can Do Anything

Living a healthy life for as long as we're blessed to live is, to me, one of the biggest challenges and greatest responsibilities we have as human beings. A mother in one of my stress management seminars said it so clearly, "I never thought about my health until it was taken away. It wasn't until I had a heart attack that I realized I had so much control over my own health. I started fighting like hell to live and found a new woman inside me—strong, brave, and determined to get well. When you lose your health, you lose everything. When you have your health, you can do anything."

> *It began as a mystery, and it will end in mystery. But what a savage and beautiful country lies in between.*
> —DIANE ACKERMAN, *A Natural History of the Senses*

Activities to Do with Your Mom

- ❑ Walk wherever your legs will take you: in the woods, the mall, the mountains, the beach, around the block, around the house.
- ❑ Join a gym together, and help each other strength-train.
- ❑ Hire and share a personal trainer.
- ❑ Take a class together in yoga, tai chi, meditation, healthy cooking, massage.

❑ Play sports—tennis, golf, bicycling, or something else that gets you moving.

❑ Relax together at a weekend spa, and treat each other to a massage.

Questions for Your Mom

• Tell me everything you know about your health history, starting with your childhood.

• Tell me everything about Dad's health history and my grandparents' medical conditions.

• Is there any history of

Addictions: Alcoholism? Cirrhosis of the liver? Drug abuse?

Allergies: Asthma? Drug allergies? Food allergies?

Bones: Osteoporosis?

Cancer: What kind?

Heart: High or low blood pressure? Heart disease? Stroke?

Immune system: HIV? Candidiasis? Chronic fatigue? Lupus? Multiple sclerosis?

Mental illness: Depression? Anxiety? Panic attacks? Migraine headaches? Schizophrenia? Manic depression?

Reproductive system: Gynecological problems? Bladder infections? Fibroids? Ovarian cysts? Yeast infections? Breast cysts? Hysterectomy? Oophorectomy (ovaries removed)?

Surgeries: Gallstones? Kidney stones? Heart bypass?

Weight: Obesity? Anorexia? Bulimia?

• What medications are you taking now?

• Are you allergic to any medications? Which ones?

• Have you ever seen a therapist? A psychiatrist? Taken antidepressants or antianxiety medication? Has anyone else in the family? Have you ever felt suicidal? If so, what was going on in your life?

• Are you taking any vitamins or supplements? What are they? What is the dosage? What are they for?

- When did you start menstruating? What were your periods like? Did you ever have PMS?
- How did you learn about menstruation? Did you and your mother ever talk about it?
- When did you start menopause? What symptoms did you experience? Was it different from what you expected? How old were you when you finished?
- What is your health insurance company and phone number? Your ID number?
- Who is your doctor? What is his or her phone number? Who are your other doctors?
- When was the last time you had a Pap smear? Mammogram? Colonoscopy? Bone scan? Blood work? When is your next appointment scheduled? Would you like me to go with you and be your secretary?
- Would you write a letter of permission giving me access to your health records if that became necessary?
- How would you like to be cared for if you became seriously ill?
- Would you like some help with meal planning and food preparation?
- What kind of exercise are you doing? Would you like to work out a reasonable exercise plan with me?
- What concerns you the most about your health?
- If you became seriously ill, how would you like me to respond?
- Is there anything I can do to help you be healthier?

Pennies from Heaven

Money

Much has changed in the world of money since our mothers were born, but two things remain the same: having money is still better than not having money, and personal money matters continue to be a taboo topic of conversation. Given a choice, most people would rather talk about their favorite sexual position than how much money they made or spent in the past year. My friend Jean Hermsen, a retired financial expert and one of the first women to start a women's banking program in the United States in the 1970s, said, "More than anything else, money can tear a family apart." So why talk to your mother about money if the possibility for conflict looms large on the horizon?

- Because, as Joel Gray sang in *Cabaret*, the hit Broadway musical, "Money makes the world go round," and the savvier both you and your mother are about money, the easier your lives will be.
- Because your mother's financial security, or lack of it, affects her future and could directly affect yours someday. Women live to an average age of eighty-five and, if married, an average of eight years longer than their husbands do. Their social security payments, pensions, and investments are significantly lower than men's are. In 1997, 19 percent of single elderly women lived below the annual poverty line of $7,698.
- Because when you understand your mother's beliefs and behaviors around money, and your own, you'll better understand yourself and make better choices in your life.
- Because money is meant to be celebrated and enjoyed.

The Past Holds the Key to Your Financial Future

Before you talk with your mother, recall your money memories and be clear about your own beliefs regarding your financial situation and your mother's. Money guru Suze Orman states in her book, *The Nine Steps to Financial Freedom*, that your past holds the key to your financial future. She reminds us that there is usually one experience we have all had while growing up that has shaped our feelings about money, which are intricately woven into our feelings of self-worth and our success in the world.

> *Our thoughts and feelings about money are, to me,*
> *fundamental factors in determining how much money each of*
> *us will, in this lifetime, be able to create and keep.*
> —SUZE ORMAN, *The Nine Steps to*
> *Financial Freedom*

Take the One with the Pink Satin Pillow and Charge It!

Money was always a sore subject in my family. My father, an architect, made the money, and my mother, a homemaker, spent it, and neither of them very much enjoyed the experience. Dad always seemed worried about whether he could afford anything that had a price tag on it, and Mom anguished about how Dad would respond when he found out how much she spent. As in many other families, the details of money were not discussed in our family while we were growing up.

Throughout my childhood, after every annual shopping expedition for school clothes, my mother's response to me was, "Go hide these clothes in your closet until school starts. We don't want your father to see them." After one shopping spree when I was eleven, I vividly remember an embarrassed store clerk telling my mother that my father had closed her charge account and she'd have to pay cash. Without saying a word but turning as red as the coat I was wearing, she grabbed my hand, turned around, and walked out. We took the bus home in silence.

That memory came shouting back the day after my mother died. I was five days away from my thirty-eighth birthday. My father, brother, two sisters, and I walked through the casket room in the basement of the funeral home where my mother's memorial service was going to be held the next day. We were told by the funeral director to take our time picking out a casket that would let my mother rest comfortably in eternal peace. Oak? Steel? Mahogany? $1,500? $3,000? $30,000? I remember looking at the price tags hanging by strings on the casket handles and thinking, "I feel like I'm shopping for furniture." Suddenly I was a child again, worrying about how Dad was going to react to paying for yet another of my mother's expenses. I half-imagined Mom walking into the room with a heavenly smile on her face, handing my father her Boston Store charge card, and saying, "Oh, for Pete's sake, Bob, take the one with the pink satin pillow and charge it!"

> *Money isn't everything; your health is the other ten percent.*
> —LILLIAN DAY, *Kiss and Tell*

Mom and I rarely talked about money except to lament that we both wished that we had more and that Dad were more comfortable spending it. This was never more evident than Mom's first shopping expedition following her spinal surgery when she was in her sixties. I took her out to buy a new pair of eyeglasses. We found a beautiful pair with gold rims and peach tinting that wouldn't look like the bottoms of Coke bottles (this worried her). When she looked at herself in the mirror, she let out a squeal of delight and said, 'I'm a new woman!' However, when the price came up—$289—she took them off and said disappointedly, "Your father will never pay for these." I asked how much he would pay for. She responded, "No more than $100." The change in her personality was dramatic. I felt terrible for her, and so angry that she had no control in her financial life. I hesitated for only a second, wondering what my father would say, and then declared, "I'll pay for half. Dad's got to have an extra $50 somewhere!" I took out my charge card and paid the first installment (not recognizing that I was continuing my mother's pattern of assuming that the money would come from somewhere besides my own efforts). When her eyewear was ready, I explained, she could return with my father to make the final payment.

I was hesitant to take a role in my parents' personal affairs, especially about money, because it was such a loaded topic for all of us, but it was hard to stay silent. I sensed that Dad wasn't buying Mom what she wanted—not so much because he couldn't afford it but because he resented her for the life they weren't able to live because of what her health problems cost him financially and emotionally.

When we arrived back at their house and she told him the news, the $100 was still too much money to my dad. Mom accepted his answer and withdrew into the bedroom (for a Hershey's bar, I'm sure). Not willing to let the issue slide, I jumped in, pleading with him to let her have a few moments of joy in her life after everything she'd been through with the surgery. The next time I saw her, she was wearing the glasses, as she did until the last time I saw her smiling, her head lying on her pink satin pillow.

Nobody Looks After You Like You Think They'll Look After You

Money is a lightning rod for underlying family issues. Whether families are rich, poor, or somewhere in between, conversations about money are likely to be complex, thorny, and difficult. Jean Hermsen, whom we met earlier in the chapter, is passionate about women taking control of their finances. She believes that "nobody looks after you like you think they'll look after you." Her husband, Hermie, died suddenly following a heart attack when he was fifty-five.

Jean suggests that when talking about money to your mother, "Be really careful, because some mothers can see your questions as prying." She recommends starting a conversation on insurance, a relatively more innocuous subject than asking your mother what her net worth is. Jean explains, "You don't really need to know how much money she has as much as you need to know she does have the necessary insurance—health and long term care—as she grows older, and enough money to cover her living expenses. Medicare kicks in at age sixty-five, and if she has severe financial problems combined with illness, she can apply for Medicaid."

Over the years Jean heard horror stories about women whose husbands died and who were left with either a confusion of papers or no insurance and mounting debt, who had to sell their home, move in with their children, or downsize to a tiny apartment to pay for their retirement years.

"Women have got to take responsibility for their own money," Jean advises, "and stop being scared of thinking that if they bring up the subject of money their husbands or parents will think they're just waiting for them to die. If they don't, they could lose everything that they and their families have worked so hard to protect."

I urge you to discuss your mother's financial situation with her. You and your mother both deserve peace of mind and financial security as you grow older.

If the Creditors Aren't Knocking at Her Door, She Must Be Doing a Good Job

Lori, an artist and married mother of a two-year-old, was twenty-eight when her father died. Six years later, her older sister, Diane, died of ovarian cancer. Following Diane's death, her mother, Fran, asked Lori to be the executor of her own estate and gave her power of attorney. Fran chose not to disclose the specifics of her financial affairs, but she made it clear she is financially secure. Lori is a co-signer on the safe deposit box and has a key to it, plus a list of her mother's insurance companies and bank accounts on computer. (States vary in who has access to a safe deposit box following the owner's death. Check with your attorney.) Fran has her finances in order and has been very clear about her wishes. If she were to become ill or, as difficult as it is to acknowledge, when she dies, she has made it easier on her daughter. Lori will be able to focus her energies on helping her mother heal or making Fran's last days more comfortable rather than stressing over money issues. In the event of Fran's death, Lori will be able to give her full attention to her own grieving process, not to how she will pay off Fran's bills.

What Do I Need to Know Before I Talk with Mom About Money?

If your mother is not as organized or open about her financial situation as Jean or Fran, what can you do? And how do you know for sure that your mother's measurement of financial security is accurate? You are not responsible for your mother's financial health, but you want to make sure she can take care of herself until her death. If she can't, you need to be prepared with a plan.

Make a list in your journal of what you know about your mother's current financial situation and how you feel about it. Think about the way she talks about and spends money now. Include your answers to these questions.

- Are you confident she can provide for herself?
- Do you have proof that she is financially secure?
- If it were necessary, would you be willing to support her entirely? Not at all? Contribute only what you can comfortably afford?
- How much could you afford to give her if she needed money now?
- Is she handling her finances successfully? Does she have a financial planner? An attorney? A will?
- Has she ever initiated a conversation with you or one of your siblings about money and her future?
- If you've talked before about money, what has the outcome been?
- How good are you at handling your finances?

Plan Your Opening Remarks

Now that you have a sense of your own thoughts and feelings about your mother's money, it's a good idea to plan your opening remarks. I don't suggest just jumping right in and saying, "What are your wishes upon your death?" This bold approach could alienate or depress her. She might be insulted if you assume she can't provide for herself or ask directly about how she plans to pay for her final years. It's quite possible, too, that she could be offended because she thinks your questions are an indication that you're waiting for her to die so you can collect your inheritance.

Begin by considering all the different springboards that could give you the jump into a helpful conversation: the death of a friend or neighbor (hers or yours), religious or memorial services, or a visit to a cemetery. When the opportunity arises, start by saying something like this: "Mom, when Jane's mom died, Jane ended up having to deal with all this financial stuff that sounded really confusing and pretty scary to me. It got me thinking about you. I know this may not be comfortable to talk about, but what are your wishes upon your death?" The perfect response from your mother would be something like: "Everything is in order, and in fact, it's all here waiting for you to review. Would you like to go through it together now?" But of course we all know that that is not usually the case. If you think your mother will resist you, consider these opening remarks: "Mom, I know this is a really touchy subject, and it may seem like I'm prying, but I've been reading all these horror stories about senior citizens who lose all their money to insurance and investment scams, and I just want to make sure you'll always be safe. I'd really appreciate it if we could talk about your financial situation.

Pause here and watch for her reaction. If she becomes uncomfortable (her body shifts, her pupils dilate, she frowns), pause and say, "Sometime. Would you be willing to do that?"

If she remains comfortable, continue on and say, "Would now be a good time?"

Wait for her answer. Let her feel that she is part of the decision. If she says no, say, "Okay. Thanks for thinking about it."

If she says yes, say, "Thanks, Mom I don't need to know how much money you have unless you want to tell me, but I would like to make sure your finances are secure and in order. How about if we sit down next Saturday and go through these things? I've got this great book that describes all the things we need to be aware of, and I'll bring that along, or if you like, I'll give it to you to read first."

What You Need to Discuss with Your Mother Regarding Finances and Health Care

Now that you've got her attention, what are the basic elements that you want to make sure you cover? Every financial planner I've talked with has offered the same advice regarding what you need to know about your mother's preparations for financial and health care security:

- A written will, preferably drafted by an attorney but at the very least reviewed by one. No matter how small her estate, a will is extremely important in making sure your mother's wishes are carried out. In many cases, a *trust* may be a better alternative than a will, as it avoids probate and is not open for public viewing. Check with your attorney for the best option.
- Long-term care insurance; one of the best ways to protect your mother if she has serious health problems and needs to go to a nursing home. This insurance will pay her expenses until her death if she must enter a nursing home for health reasons.
- A living will (also called a health care directive or declaration, depending on the state you live in) to protect her if she is suddenly incapacitated. A living will tells your mother's physician specifically what to do if she becomes incapacitated (unable to speak for herself).
- A durable power of attorney for health care (in some states called a living will), which lets your mother designate a specific person to make medical decisions for her if she is incapacitated. It also allows that person to decide what kind of care she should receive. In the absence of this document or of a living will, your mother's physician has the final authority on how to treat her.
- A durable power of attorney for finances, which allows your mother to designate someone to make her financial decisions should she become incapacitated. This document and the durable power of attorney for health care are different from the simple power of attorney in that they protect your mother if she is incapacitated, whereas the

simple power of attorney doesn't, but is useful when she doesn't have the time to handle her affairs, is having an operation, or is going on a long vacation.

If you know your mother is not savvy about money or has no interest in the financial details of her life, it's important to find a way to help her be more financially responsible to herself or risk losing not only her home but also her independence and self-worth. You can start by suggesting she make a detailed list of her income and expenses and then calculate how much money she'll need on a yearly basis until at least age eighty-five. From there, read Suze Orman's book *The Nine Steps to Financial Freedom*, in particular "Step 4—Being Responsible to Those You Love," as well as her book *The Courage to Be Rich*, specifically Chapter 12, "The Courage to Live After a Death," for more specific details on helping your mother manage her money.

Other information sources that you can both benefit from are the Internet, which has several on-line support communities that offer financial information; your local community college, bank, or investment firm, which may hold classes; and women's business and health care conferences that generally offer sessions on financial matters.

Living with Your Mother Is a Viable Financial Option

Besides living with your mother, other options are possible: starting an investment club together, getting personally involved in your mother's finances by hiring a bookkeeper, managing her money yourself with her direction, or helping her spend it (just kidding). But some women are finding that inviting their mothers to live with them is a viable financial option that is helpful to both of them. Karen, a massage therapist, and her mother, Looey, a retiree, have created a unique living arrangement that has brought Looey emotional support and physical care and has given Karen financial relief.

Looey was living alone in her big home in Arizona when she became seriously ill. Karen, owning a home and a business in California, was in the midst of a financial crisis and in serious debt. After much discussion, Looey sold her house and moved in with Karen. Looey loaned money from the sale of her house to Karen at 10 percent interest to pay off her debt. Karen pays her back on a monthly basis by deducting rent from her mother for living in her house. As I talked with both women, I was encouraged by their easy laughter and obvious affection for each other and the creative way they handled their finances. Looey explains, "We have a great deal of respect for each other. We're totally different. I like to tidy the kitchen and make my bed—" Karen laughs and finishes Looey's sentence, "and I never make my bed." Their easy exchange continued with Looey laughing once again when she said, "We go halves on groceries. I keep a running total, and sometimes I mess it up and have to start over from scratch." You can hear the smile in Karen's voice when she says, "That's okay with me."

Money Can Be Fun

Jean Hermsen said it best: "If women could only see that managing money can be fun. Keeping records and watching your money grow is fun! And any woman can do it at any age if she's willing to learn. Tell daughters to buy their mothers stock for their birthdays and join an investment club together. Discuss, talk, share ideas. There's so much to learn and enjoy about money if they'll just decide to be interested. It's a choice, just like anything else in life."

> *Prosperity is the natural result of opening our minds to our creative imaginations and being willing to act on our ideas.*
> —RUTH ROSS, *Prospering Woman*

Activities to Do with Your Mom

❑ Join or start an investment club.
❑ Buy your mother a book on money and investing:

- *The Nine Steps to Financial Freedom*, by Suze Orman
- *The Courage to Be Rich*, by Suze Orman
- *Prince Charming Isn't Coming: How Women Get Smart About Money*, by Barbara Stanny
- *The Energy of Money: A Spiritual Guide to Financial and Personal Fulfillment*, by Maria Nemeth
- *10 Smart Money Moves for Women: How to Conquer Your Financial Fears*, by Judith Briles

❑ Treat your mother to a magazine subscription with personal finance information, such as *Money* or *Modern Maturity*.

❑ Check out on-line finance Web sites—for example, *www.fool.com, www.etrade.com, www.pathfinder.com/money*.

❑ Buy shares of stock for your mother for her birthday.

Questions for Your Mom

- What are some of the biggest lessons you've learned about money?
- What is one of the dominant money memories from your childhood?
- What beliefs about money have most shaped the way you spend money?
- How did your parents handle money? Who paid the bills?
- What did you do with your money? Did you save? Spend?
- What kind of insurance do you carry, and what are the company names and policy numbers? Health? Life? Long-term care? Disability (if self-employed)?
- What are your financial plans for retirement?
- Do you have a financial guide or a person to whom you look for financial advice? What is this person's name? Phone number?
- Have you assigned durable power of attorney to anyone yet?
- Do you have a will?
- Do you have a safe deposit box? What bank? Where is your safe deposit box key? Who are the authorized signers besides you?
- Who is your attorney? What is this person's phone number?

- What is the most enjoyable gift you've ever bought for yourself? For someone else?
- What's the most money you've ever spent on something?
- If you won the lottery, how much would you want to win, and how would you spend it?

You Are So Beautiful

Self-Image and Beauty

In the ten years I spent as a professional image consultant, I worked with over 6,000 people, mostly women, in private or small group sessions. My mission was to help people, in particular women, project a more positive, powerful, and polished presence. At least half of these meetings included adult daughters and their mothers. Sometimes Grandma was included, and often Aunt Jane and Cousin Julie. Our time together always started off with a discussion of the superficial aspects of appearance and how to improve it (what color lipstick to wear based on your "season," how to make foundation last longer, how to look ten pounds slimmer) and often ended with profound conversation on the emotional and societal implications of body image and aging (feelings of loss and depression after a mastectomy; the shame in being overweight; being discriminated against for being heavy, beautiful, not beautiful enough, or too old). If we were lucky enough to get to the deeper issues and speak of them in a curious, nonjudgmental, and compassionate way, there was laughter, honesty, intimacy, and celebration between all of us.

Rewriting Your Mother's Job Description

Most women I've talked with over the years said their mothers do not discuss their most intimate feelings about their body image with them. The conversation is kept at a superficial level directed toward the daughter—"You look nice today," "That's a nice outfit on you," "Where did you get those earrings?"—but the air is filled with lots of unspoken gestures and innuendos. I'm not saying not to talk about superficial things. Talking about clothes and makeup is a fun part of being a woman. What I am saying is to go deeper. Your mother's job description hasn't included the right to reveal to you how she feels about her body, good or bad, or for that matter, how she generally feels about herself. Her task of guiding you toward womanhood has been more about telling you what to do and how to look. Those rules need to be changed as we grow into women. If your mother isn't able to recognize and shift this energy, then you, as her daughter, can help her do so. But first we have to look at what beliefs are holding either or both of you back.

Three Myths That Prevent Effective Communication About Body Image

There are three myths that get in the way of effective communication about beauty and self-image with your mother. Read through them and see if any of these has kept you or your mother from sharing a closer relationship:

- If a mother shares openly her concerns and disappointments about her own body, she loses her daughter's respect and teaches her daughter not to like her own body.
- If a mother acknowledges directly her own pleasure with her appearance, especially if she (or her daughter) thinks her daughter isn't as attractive as herself, the mother makes her daughter feel inadequate by comparison and may even invite competition.
- It's impossible to have a meaningful conversation about appearance because either the mother or the daughter (or both) is too critical or sensitive about her appearance.

The truth is that open, intimate communication between a mother and her adult daughter about how each feels about her appearance can be very enlightening and healing, *if* the conversation is approached in a curious, nonjudgmental, compassionate way. Much of the criticism that flows back and forth between mothers and daughters is because one or both women are caught in the "You should [dye your roots, lose weight, stop being so self-absorbed]" dialogue instead of the "I feel [uncomfortable with the way *I* look; helpless when you complain about your appearance but don't do anything to change yourself]" or "I wonder [how our beliefs about beauty and aging compare, what you've learned about the meaning of beauty over the years]."

One of the Things I Really Like About Being a Woman

Before you talk with your mom, it's a good idea to review your beliefs about your self-image, your mother's image, and the influence she's had on your personal style. Personal appearance is a sensitive topic. You want to be clear about how you feel so that you can articulate your thoughts clearly and calmly to her. You also want to know what you want from her after you tell her your memories and feelings. Do you want an apology, a hug, or simply that she know you appreciate her support or that it was hard for you to smile when you looked in the mirror after she told you how fat you were?

Take a moment to respond to these statements in your journal:

- One of the things I really like about being a woman is . . .
- One message about beauty or self-image I've received from my mother is . . .
- The physical qualities I've inherited from my mother are . . .
- One aspect of my mother's appearance I like is . . .
- One aspect of my appearance I like is . . .
- When I think about my body growing older, I . . .
- If I were easier on myself about the way I look, I'd . . .
- I get my sense of self-worth from . . .
- One thing I feel very strongly about regarding a woman's self-image and appearance is . . .

Answering these questions will give you more insight into what you are and are not comfortable thinking about or talking about regarding your appearance. If you're like most other women, you probably found yourself feeling a variety of thoughts and emotions—some of them pleasant, some of them not, some of them your own, some of them your mother's voice in your head. We don't often explore the thoughts behind our feelings about our self-image, and when we do, we sometimes find out that what we thought was our issue is really our mother's issue, and vice versa. We notice that we have taken on beliefs of our mother that no longer serve us. Or we find out just the opposite: our mother's beliefs are sound, and we would do well to follow her advice now that we better understand our own perspective. And if we're really lucky, we share similar thoughts with our mother; when we have differences, we accept and learn from them. Once you've finished this topic, I encourage you to ask your mother to respond to the above statements. If you've never talked with your mother before about body issues, when you talk with her, I suggest the following process:

1. Say, "Mom, I've been thinking about the different messages women get about the way they look. I answered some questions in this book I've been reading and I began to wonder what you'd say. If you'll answer them too, we can compare notes and learn more about each other." Keep your voice and words upbeat.

2. If she is resistant to the idea, suggest that you make a copy of the statements, and let her answer them in her own time and share her answers with you in writing. If she likes the idea of sharing, tell her that you will read through each statement and ask her to respond with her first thoughts. Before you comment on her answers or share your own, finish all the statements with her. This will keep you and your mother focused on her process and give you time to think about which information you want to discuss when she's finished.

3. Thank her for sharing her thoughts with you when you finish and offer some form of praise to her for being willing to be vulnerable and open with you: "Mom, thanks for doing this. I know some of the questions were hard to answer, so I really appreciate your being willing to tell me more about yourself."

4. Go back and review each statement together, comparing your responses and using them as points of discussion. Remember to stay focused in "I" language—"I feel . . . ," "I'm surprised by . . . ," "I appreciate that you. . . ." Using the word "I" helps keep you focused on yourself and your feelings, prevents blame, and sets a pattern for your mother to do the same.

Good Genes

When Sue approached her mother about answering the statements on appearance, her mother was initially resistant. Sue gently persisted, telling her that she was excited to share her own responses because she realized how much she had gained from her mother. Without pausing she continued, "Like this one—'The physical qualities I've inherited from my mother are good genes!' Thanks, Mom." Her mother laughed and said, "What else is on that list?" Together they went through the list. At the end of their conversation, Sue's mother said, "I never thought it was appropriate to talk about myself this way with you. Not only has it made me feel closer to you, but it's made me more aware of the good influence I've had on you. I wish my mother were here so we could do this with her."

Beauty Is Womb Deep

In one image session, I remember going to the home of a young woman named Bonnie, who had included her mother, grandmother, aunt, and her mother's best friend at our session. As each woman introduced herself, I asked her to describe a recent success, however small, in her life. Bonnie, a petite, trim, twenty-four-year-old teacher, began: "I lost ten pounds." When I congratulated her, all the women broke into hearty laughter. I was confused, not understanding the laughter. Bonnie noticed the perplexed look on my face and grinned, saying, "Five pounds in each breast. I used to be a 34EE. I had breast reduction surgery. When I told my husband I was doing it, he left me. I was devastated, but it's the best thing that ever happened to me. I couldn't have gone through it without my mom and my grandma encouraging me. They kept telling me no man is worth losing my self-esteem for." All the women broke out in applause as Bonnie finished speaking.

I learned again and again how powerful a mother's words—or silence—are in shaping our sense of self. We need her reassurance. We also need her truth. Truly, beauty is more than skin deep; *beauty is womb deep.*

She's a Recovering *Leave It to Beaver* Mom

Tami, a social worker and mother of two teenage boys, describes her mother as a recovering *Leave It to Beaver* mom. "I started dying my hair the first time I saw gray show up when I was in my twenties. She didn't start until she turned fifty-five. She didn't think it was right to spend money on hair dye, but she'd never go out of the house without makeup on. Still won't. I hardly wear any. Never have, never will. We're real different that way. But we can talk about anything. I have problems going up and down weight wise, and she's never made me feel bad about it. She's always said there's more to a person than that and emphasized my outgoing personality. 'Oh you're so lucky you're so outgoing and you can talk to people,' she says. She's always made me feel really good about myself.

"When one of Mom's friends was diagnosed with breast cancer and lost a breast, it devastated her. I asked her, 'What would you do if it happened to you?' She said, 'Take 'em both.' She's not vain that way. When another friend had a facelift, she mentioned it to me in a phone call. I asked her if she'd ever consider having it done. She said, 'No, it's not worth the pain or the time it takes to heal. Besides, I've earned every wrinkle on my face.' She feels pretty good about herself and is happier than she's ever been. I really admire her."

Tami's relationship with her mother had deepened when her mother gave up the June Cleaver "perfect mother" facade that was so familiar in the 1950s and 1960s. While there is nothing wrong with a mother wanting to present a wholesome and attractive image to her family and the public, when that is all others experience of her, she denies herself the joy of being seen, known, and appreciated for who she really is. She creates a myth instead of a relationship.

How do you create the safety, support, and understanding that Tami shares with her mother? You start simply and lightheartedly talking about new clothing purchases, makeup tips, or famous women whose style you admire. You pay your mother a compliment about her new earrings or her hair. Slowly you move toward deeper and more meaningful issues about how your mother feels when she sees her body getting older. You invite your mother's opinion, you ask questions about how she responded in a similar situation that you're facing now, and you welcome your differences as learning opportunities about yourself.

Helping a Critical Mother Shift from Your Image to Her Feelings

If your mother tends toward criticism about your image, I still recommend talking with her, but focus your conversation on her feelings about herself. This may be exactly what it takes to break the pattern and bring balance into your relationship. Sometimes, though, to open that door, you need to set boundaries with her about the feedback she gives you about your image.

Author Geneen Roth provides an excellent example of how to do this. In her book *Breaking Free from Compulsive Eating*, she writes about an exchange with her mother concerning her weight: "Not long ago I spent a few days with her in New York. On the second day my mother said, 'I'm going to tell you something and I hope it doesn't make you upset, but you've gained weight. I can see it in your legs.'

"When I felt myself panicking, I went for a walk and got back in touch with my feelings about my body, how much I truly liked it, and that I thought it looked fine. Rounder, but still fine. On my walk I realized that I was still all the things I was before I'd gained the five pounds and that life was still as lovely and painful as it always had been. On my walk I realized that I wasn't fat. And I realized that my mother, at fifty-two, with a thin, shapely body, still thinks she's fat. Back at the house, I went to my mother, who was sitting at the round linoleum table. I said, 'Mom, I know you meant well, but please: Don't make any comments about my weight. It's too painful.' And I haven't heard a whisper on the subject again."

Geneen Roth set successful limits with her mother. You can too. If you have a history of too much focus on your problems, rather than on your mother's feelings about herself, establish clear boundaries with your mother. The next time she begins to criticize your appearance (or anything else), use this mutually supportive four-step technique:

1. Take a deep breath (or a break, if necessary) and mentally center yourself with soothing thoughts of encouragement. "I am a good person, and what is most important is what I think of myself. I'm an adult and I give myself permission to set limits with Mom."
2. Acknowledge her positive intention. "I know you meant well . . ."
3. Declare what you want. ". . . But please: Don't make any comments about . . ." (describe your problem: weight, hair, makeup, relationship, work, etc.).
4. Tell her how you feel. "It's too painful."

If you are repeatedly on the receiving end of a critical conversation you can set more specific limits to handle the pain. Use your pain to shift the focus and deepen the conversation by reinforcing what you want:

"Our relationship is important to me and I want us to be able to talk about difficult things like this, but I need a different framework. In the future, if you feel the need to talk about my weight issues, tell me how you feel about yourself and your weight, and what feelings come up for you about yourself when you see me. Then maybe I'll feel freer to acknowledge your concerns and we'll both feel more supported and closer to each other."

This gives both you and your mother breathing space, gives your mother the opportunity to look at her own issues if she chooses, and opens the door to more meaningful conversation in the future.

> *I do not live in my thighs or my droopy butt. I live in joy and motion and cover-ups.*
> —ANNE LAMOTT, *Traveling Mercies*

That Toilet Paper Thing You Do with Your Hair

I never outwardly heard my mother diminish her body except for wishing she could get rid of her jowls and crepey neck and keep her weight under control. She loved to shop for clothes and had two six-foot closets full of three different sizes of clothing. If I were a therapist, I'd say that she developed a clothing addiction to help her cope with her depression and my father's difficult personality. Her weekly hair and nail appointment at the Edgewood Beauty Salon was as much an escape as it was a beauty treatment. The first two nights after her hair-style was freshly (and stiffly) styled, she wrapped her head in toilet paper, looking as if she was wearing a papier-mâché beehive on her head. (Now isn't that a sexy image. I can just hear my father saying, "Oh, Grace, would you please do that toilet paper thing with your hair again. It really turns me on.") She continued this ritual until she died with the exception of one month when I was in my late twenties. Dad was trying to cut costs and told Mom that her weekly salon trips were being cut and she'd have to do her own hair. She accepted his decision, believing that his word was law, and set to doing her own hair.

The first week was a complete disaster, but Dad told her she'd get better at it. The second week there was no improvement, so Dad suggested she call me to help her. She did, in tears. Angry at his insensitive behavior but wanting to help her, I said, "Sure, Mom. How about if I cut and perm it too? I've watched enough hairstylists cut hair, and I just saw that new machine on TV that sucks your hair into a vacuum and cuts it perfectly." Dad dropped her off, and we went shopping for hair perm products and the vacuum cutting machine.

The stores were out of the cutting machine, so we bought a box of 'Toni Natural Wave' perming solution and went back to my house for an afternoon beauty salon party. Two hours later, when I was rolling a piece of perm rod paper around her hair for the hundredth time, I was ready to quit. Three hours later, I knew I was in trouble when I had to cut shorter and shorter chunks of the same hair to match what I'd just finished cutting. When I finished five hours later and gave her a mirror to look at her new haircut, perm, and style, her eyebrows jumped up to the top of her forehead and her eyeballs bulged out like the black molly fish in our childhood aquarium. She coughed, trying to hide her shock. For a second we both stood there speechless, and then she laughed and didn't stop until she doubled over. When she recovered she said, "Well, if I'd known this was what it would take to convince your father to let me go back to the beauty parlor, I'd have called you three weeks ago."

Hairy Apes, Ugly Ducklings, and Swans

A very big part of my mother's beauty to me was her laughter. Her sense of humor comforted me through many nights of tears during my growing-up years. While I know there were happy moments, my memories of sixth, seventh, and eighth grade are more often filled with running from the taunts of peers, mostly boys, on the way to and from school. I was tomboy with a big crook in my nose and feet as big as the floor tiles in the school hallway. I was flat chested and string bean tall. My arms were so hairy that when the boys saw me, they'd shout at the top of their lungs, "Look, there goes the flat-chested hairy ape." One particularly brutal day, I remember running the entire four blocks home, and bursting into tears as I opened the front door and saw my mother. After spilling my story, she told me that boys teased her the same way when she was my age. "They called me 'Four-Eyes,' " she said, "because I wore glasses, and 'Greasy Grace' because my thin hair laid so flat on my head." She said she cried just like me, but her mother taught her to laugh it off. She promised me that one day I'd "blossom," the hair on my arms would fade away, and that even though I felt like the ugly duckling, someday I would look in the mirror and see a beautiful swan.

Her words wrapped around me like a hug. I repeated her promise like a chanting Buddhist as I grew by an inch or two every summer, reaching my final height of five feet ten inches in my early twenties. By then, my feet had grown to a size ten and continue to expand—size twelve as I write. As I've grown older, the hair on my arms has faded away just like Mom said. The only thing that's blossomed, though, is the rose bush on my balcony. It's hard not to notice cleavage on the beach, but for me the health issues outweigh any satisfaction I'd gain from artificially blooming my breasts. Some days I look in the mirror and catch a glimpse of a swan, and some days I hear a lot of quacking. I've learned to smile; I hear my mother: "Look at that beautiful long neck."

To seek after beauty as an end is a wild goose chase, a will-o'-wisp, because it is to misunderstand the very nature of beauty, which is the normal condition of a thing being as it should.
—ADA BETHUNE, in Judith Stoughton,
Proud Donkey of Schaerbeek

Activities to Do with Your Mom

- ☐ Shopping
- ☐ Spa weekend, pajama party
- ☐ Beauty salon afternoon—hair style and manicure, department store makeover
- ☐ Wardrobe consulting session

Questions to Ask Your Mom

- What do you like about being a woman?
- Where do you get your sense of self-worth?
- What is one message about beauty or self-image you received from your mother?
- What physical qualities did you inherit from your mother?
- What do you like about your mother's appearance? Your own? Mine?
- If you were easier on yourself about the way you look, what would you do differently?
- What do you like about the way you look? What would you change?
- What is your favorite perfume? Favorite hairstyle? Beauty tip?
- What's one of your favorite outfits? What's the sexiest outfit you've ever worn?
- What's been one of your favorite hairstyles?
- How do you *really* feel about plastic surgery?
- What woman's style do you most admire?
- What's the weirdest beauty treatment you've done?
- What do you think about the way women my age express their beauty today versus the way you did when you were my age?
- What have you learned about beauty and aging?

Some Enchanted Evening

Romantic Intimacy and Men

Of all the conversations that are sure to arouse joy, suffering, confusion, fear, frustration, satisfaction, tears, laughter, and bliss, it's the topic of romantic relationships and all the roles they play in our life: crush, date, unrequited love, boyfriend, partner, husband, ex-husband, old flame, new flame, friend, lover.

Our mother is no exception to this rule. Whether she gave birth to you or adopted you, she has experienced a few things about love and marriage that she may not have shared with you. Yes, she may have offered her wisdom, criticism, and advice to you about your relationships, but she may also have kept much of her personal experience of loving to herself. That's a story you want to know more about.

> *A successful marriage requires falling in love many times—always with the same person.*
> —MIGNON MCLAUGHLIN, *The Second Neurotic's Notebook*

I will be the first to admit that talking about all the different aspects of romantic intimacy with one's mother can be daunting. At first I hesitated to include the topic in this book, but I felt compelled to do so because of what I learned in my research. The more willing we are to talk about romantic intimacy with our mothers—how both of us express it, what it means to us, how it makes us feel, the cultural rules and taboos—the safer and more loving our world will be for future generations of daughters.

As you begin to explore your mother's experiences of romantic love, whether it is dating, marriage, sex, or perhaps divorce or widowhood, you may find that she's not the woman you thought she was. You could discover, as I did, that your mother is much more—more interesting, more sensual, more flirtatious, or courageous—and a woman you can now relate to on a whole new level.

I think you'll agree that it's easier to talk to friends about their love life than your mother. Our culture has a place for mothers, and in most cases this place doesn't include talking openly about the passionate aspects of how she got to be a mother, how she's managed to keep the lover alive inside her marriage, and how she's dealt with intimacy issues in her relationship. I realize that talking about these things could be embarrassing or even painful, but the rewards are tremendous. The more we know about our mother's romantic experiences, the more we are able to understand ourselves. Your mother influences all the ways you smile, flirt, touch, kiss, and do that marvelous and complex mating dance.

If your mother and father shared a respectful, loving, and nurturing marriage, your conversation will include a pleasant trip down memory lane. As well, you'll want to ask what your mother has done to keep her marriage and herself happy. If your parents' relationship was less than perfect and your parents either stayed in an unhappy marriage or divorced, you'll want to acknowledge the sadness and disappointment you both most likely felt as a result but not dwell on it. Even a bad marriage has good times and learning times. What was the deciding factor in your mother's marrying your father? What did she model or change from her own parents' marriage? What did she do when she sensed love slipping away? Did she see a marriage counselor? How did she keep herself going? The idea here is to understand your mother's experience of love—and your own—and to celebrate the mystery of romance.

Your Mother's Love Legacy

What love legacy has your mother bestowed on you? What memories, messages, and meanings about love have you absorbed from her? Before talking with your mother, write a page in your journal about what you've learned from your mother about romantic love and men, or complete the following statements:

- When I was a small child and saw my mom and dad kiss, I . . .
- I first learned about sex when . . .
- When my parents argued, they resolved their conflict by . . .
- The ways that my mother showed my father she loved him included . . .
- The ways that my father showed my mother he loved her included . . .
- I remember my mom looking or acting sexy or sensual when she . . .
- The last time I talked to my mother about sex, she told me . . .
- The last time I talked to Mom about her relationship with Dad, she said . . .
- Messages I learned about men and love from my mother are . . .
- One positive love pattern I've continued from my mother is . . .

When I answered these statements, I was most surprised by the fact that I had little positive instruction from my mother (or my father) on how to express romantic love. All I could draw up in my memory were the cards my parents exchanged on Mother's Day and Father's Day, their birthdays, and their wedding anniversaries. I laughed when I realized that this one gesture—sending cards—is what I do more than anything else in my love relationships.

As I dig back into my memory and reflect on my answers, as well as those of women I interviewed, I gratefully remember more subtle expressions of love between my parents. But sadly, what I remember most about their relationship are the arguments: my father's yelling, my mother's tears, fear, and passive acceptance of my father's verbal abuse and lack of empathy. I wonder if I would think or feel differently if they were here to tell me more of their private thoughts. I imagine Mom saying, "He was a good provider. He could fix anything. He bought me a brand-new Mustang convertible for my forty-eighth birthday and that Baldwin Swinger organ for my fiftieth, and hot fudge sundaes when I was feeling blue. He stayed in our marriage when he didn't want to and supported me throughout my illnesses, and he loved you kids."

If you find yourself at a loss for memories of romantic love between your parents or your mother draws a blank when you talk with her, be gentle and patient. Remember that these aren't questions we often ask even ourselves, and the topic may be private and sensitive to your mother. It's quite possible that she will ask you why you want to know about her private matters, and if she does, you want to be prepared with an answer so that instead of stammering or drawing a blank, you can remain calm and curious. Sometimes all your mother needs to talk more about herself is a firm, clear, "Because it would help me under-stand you and myself better." If she asks you why you want to know, here are a few reasons to offer.

- "I'm interested in knowing more about you."
- "I may learn something new about you and Dad that will enrich my memory of your relationship."
- "It will answer questions I've had about the past."
- "I want to understand my own relationships better, and I've learned that the nut doesn't fall far from the tree."
- "It could be a really interesting and intimate conversation that would bring us closer."
- "It feels good to talk about happy memories." (Don't be shy about wanting to revisit positive memories. It's as comforting as hearing our favorite bedtime story or song.)

One way to begin your conversation about love and men is to ask your mother to finish the sentence completions that you worked on in your journal. You'll find out about her experiences with her mother, which makes for a safer opening to explore her relationship with your father than jumping right in with, "How's your sex life, Mom?" If she is a chatty person or very busy, going through the sentence completions in person or over the phone makes more sense. If she is a private person or enjoys writing, ask her to write her answers in your journal. Then share your answers and insights. The discussion that follows is sure to be an interesting one.

> *Personally, I like two types of men—domestic and foreign.*
> —MAE WEST, *The Wit and Wisdom of Mae West*

What Made You Decide to Marry Dad?

Another more lighthearted starting point for discussion is asking about your mother's early experiences with love. Who was her first boyfriend? Who kissed her first, and how old was she? Was she ever engaged to someone else besides your dad? How did she and your father meet? What made her decide to marry your dad?

Asking your mother what specifically helped her decide to marry your father can spark the conversational fire about men, rekindle positive memories, and add insight into your own decisions about men and marriage. Whatever choices we make about marriage—to stay single, get married, stay married, divorce—our reasons are usually complex—much more complex than what our mothers experienced. They grew up when divorce was still the exception rather than the rule. Happy or unhappy, our mothers stayed with their husbands through thick and thin and made the most of their circumstances. If our mothers have been unhappy in their marriage we want to know why they have stayed, and if they're happy we want to know how they've kept the romance alive.

Chris, a management consultant, describes her childhood as a cross between *Leave It to Beaver* and *Father Knows Best*. Her parents expressed love easily and often. They had a lot of fun, and they respected each other. I asked Chris if she would ask her mother, "What were some of the best parts of being in love with Dad?" Here is the e-mail her mother, June, sent:

I felt so loved by your father. For the most part he never said any-
thing to hurt my feelings (he knew I was I was sensitive). . . . Com-
munication is so important. This lasted all through our lives. Near
the end, a couple of years before Audie died, I remember hearing
some singing from outside as I was waking up in the morning. I
looked out the window and there was Audie on the front porch
singing, "I love you truly."

Chris's inquiry led to a loving reminiscence by her mother that captured not just stories but love lessons and memories that Chris is able
to pass on to her young adult children. Imagine how much more love
there would be in the world if we spent more time asking the question,
"What's right?" instead of "What's wrong?"

Make love, not war—hell, do both—get married.
—Bumper sticker

Why Did You Stay with Dad?

For all the problems my mother and father had in their marriage, their
resolute commitment to their marriage vows, in spite of their challenges, remains one of the strongest messages about marriage I received
from both of them. In moments of frustration, I would ask my mother,
"Why do you stay with Dad if you're so unhappy?" Her response was
always the same "I love him, and I married him for life, no matter how
he acts. He doesn't mean it. He doesn't know any better."

I didn't follow in my mother's footsteps. I divorced at age twenty-
seven, against her and my father's wishes. It was a difficult and painful
year, but I made the right decision for me.

As time passed, I became less tolerant of my father's disrespectful
behavior toward my mother. One day after I'd heard too much, I boldly
said to Mom, "Why don't you leave? I'll help you. We'll find you a little
apartment or we can live together." In her early sixties at the time, she
said, "I love your father. Besides, I can't do that. I don't have any money

or means to support myself." I couldn't argue with her feelings of love for my father and realized she was right about the support issue. I was barely making enough money to support myself, much less her. We never discussed the issue again. After a few therapy sessions, I learned that I didn't have to play the role of therapist, savior, or divorce court judge. The best thing I could do was let her vent and create more opportunities for her to enjoy herself away from my father. I said the serenity prayer a lot.

> *God grant me the serenity*
> *to accept the things I cannot change,*
> *courage to change the things I can,*
> *and wisdom to know the difference.*
> —"The Serenity Prayer"
> (Reinhold Niebuhr)

I was surprised to learn that I was not alone in this situation. As I collected questions from women in my stress management and communication seminars, I noticed a familiar question. One of the top three questions women indicated they wanted to ask their mother was, "Why did you stay with Dad?"

What's interesting to me about the question is not just your mother's answer, but also your motives for asking it. If you're like me, you already know the answer. The question is a mask for anger. For me it was anger at my mother for allowing herself to be treated so poorly, at my father for treating her so poorly, and at myself for not being able to fix the situation.

The question can also be an indirect way of stating how you really feel. If this is the case for you, I suggest you first ask yourself the question, "Why do I think Mom is staying with Dad?" Once you know the answer to that question (because she's afraid to be on her own, because she has no income, because she takes her marriage vows literally, because there are intimate details she's kept private, or some other private matter), address that issue with her. Make sure you have already established a comfortable rapport with her during a calm moment—perhaps driving in the car, or on vacation, or during a quiet afternoon walk. Start out with a comment like: "Mom, I've always wondered why you've stayed with Dad. Sometimes you seem so sad and unhappy, and that really gets to me. I'm guessing that you've stayed all these years because you're not sure how you'd earn a living on your own [or whatever reason you came up with]. Am I right?" If your mother says yes, your response might be: "That must feel pretty scary. At least it would to me. What keeps you going?" This acknowledges your feelings and continues to move the conversation in a positive direction, helping you better understand and support her.

If your mother says no and becomes defensive, your response could be: "It sounds like I've upset you, and that's not my intention. I want to understand your decisions better and help myself feel better when I see you looking so unhappy. [Do not pause here. Keep going. She'll need your guidance to stay focused.] How do you see your situation?"

Your intention is not to make your mother feel that she's made a bad choice: it's about understanding her perspective, whether or not you agree with her. Maintaining an attitude of curiosity and compassion will help keep you focused and calm. Having asked this infamous question of my mother numerous times—with a provocative, frustrated tone—I can guarantee that if you ask her the question with the same tone, you will put her on the defensive. The word *why* is a blaming word and is usually accompanied by a judgmental tone of voice that does nothing to enhance communication. If you truly do not understand why she has stayed, rephrase the question into a statement about how your mother's decision to stay with your father makes you feel and then ask her to tell you more about how she experiences the situation.

Daughter: Mom, I feel so sad and angry when I watch you and Dad interact. I know you're doing the best you can, but if I were you, I wouldn't be able to last more than two seconds in the same room with him if he talked to me like that. I wonder what's going on in your mind when he treats you like that.

Mother: Your father does the best he can. And besides I love him.

Daughter: [Compassionately] Well, Mom, I could never do what you're doing, and I just want you to know that if you ever decide that you want to get help or stop him from talking to you like that, I'll do whatever I can to help you. No one should have to live with this kind of treatment.

Your mother will make the decisions she feels are best for her, and while it may be difficult to watch, your goal is to understand her, not change her.

Six months after Terri had a conversation similar to the one above with her mother, Carol, her mother sought out therapy and began learning about how her own passive behavior contributed to her husband's verbal abuse. Carol began to see that she had the right to expect to be treated with respect, which many women of earlier generations did not believe (and still don't believe in many families and cultures). She became emotionally stronger and learned how critical a strong support system is in maintaining her health and a healthy marriage. She began to talk more with her friends and Terri about her problems. Her first big step was to define exactly what she wanted and needed. Instead of waiting for her husband to ask or decide what they would do, she'd say, "Here's what I'd like to do. What would you like to do?"

Terri's father wasn't happy with the shift in power between them and told Carol that she could not continue to use *their* money to "see a shrink." Carol didn't know how to respond, so she became quiet and retreated, as she usually did. But she did one thing differently. Instead of keeping her experience private, she called Terri and told her what had happened. Terri, having been in therapy herself, listened and then asked a brilliant question: "Mom, what do you think your therapist would tell you?"

Carol thought for a minute and said, "She'd ask me what I really want." Terry continued to probe gently: "What do you want?"

"I want to feel better about myself and I want to keep going to therapy because it helps me feel better about myself. But your father won't keep paying for it."

"Mom, it's your money too."

"Yes, but your father earned it."

"Mom, you earned it too. You've taken care of him all these years so he could work. That's worth something."

"I know, but your father doesn't see it that way."

"It sounds as if you don't see it that way either. You know, some therapists have sliding-scale fees. You might ask your therapist about that. And maybe there's a way you can earn the money." Terri laughed. "If worse comes to worst, you can do my laundry and clean my apartment, and I'll pay for your therapy."

Carol was so overwhelmed by the support she received from Terri that she broke into tears and said, "I never knew I could ask my own daughter for help. I didn't think it was right."

There are times when the above comment is appropriate, and other times when a mother (or daughter) is wise to seek outside counsel, whether it is from a friend (outside of a family member) or a therapist. And while I'm not suggesting you become your mother's therapist, I do think that guiding her toward counseling and supporting her in the process of change is an extremely loving gesture that you would do for any friend who needed help.

Why Would I Want to Talk to My Mother About Sex?

If you're like many other women, you learned about sex from one of your friends around the time you were in fourth grade. God forbid your mother ever mention the "s word" to you, which is precisely why I'm asking you to have the conversation now.

I learned about sex the summer after fourth grade from my cousin in sixth grade. I walked in on her clapping her Ken doll on top of her best friend's Barbie doll that was lying on the bed. I asked what she was doing. She said, "Making babies. Ken puts his thing in Barbie's hole, and out comes a baby nine months later." I was shocked, dashed out of the room, and ran the four blocks home to ask my mother if it was true. "Yes, but when two people do that it's because they love each other and want to have a baby." That was the last time I had that kind of conversation with her.

I was one of the last girls in my group of grade school friends to begin to menstruate. When I finally got my period at age thirteen, I excitedly and nervously told my mother. She walked me into the bathroom, gave me a sanitary belt and napkins, demonstrated the proper arrangement over my clothes, and said calmly, "You're a woman now. Do you know what that means?" I nodded my head yes, and that was the end of our talk.

That evening my father came into my bedroom to say goodnight as he usually did. But this time, much to my embarrassment, he stood at the end of my bed for the longest time (it was probably one second longer than usual) looking at me and then said matter-of-factly, "Your mother tells me you're a woman now." I threw the covers over my head and lay there still as a statue, hoping he'd go away. He did and mentioned my womanhood only twice more. The first was when I was nineteen (the same summer I discovered birth control). He said, "Don't you dare go out of the house with those yellow hot pants on. They'll get you in trouble." The second time was when I became engaged. While looking out the kitchen window, he said, "You *will* stay pure as the driven snow until you're married."

My mother and I never discussed the intimate details of any of these memories or either of our sex lives as adults; however, I think she would have if I had asked. I remember at the end of my wedding day, she sat down with me, put her hand on top of mine, and said, "Honey, tonight when you go up to your hotel room with your husband, you may not like it, but just do what he says. It will be over soon." Everything I needed to know about my mother's feelings about sex came through in those few sentences. I wished I had felt comfortable enough to tell her that while I felt guilty about having gone against every moral principle I'd been raised with, I enjoyed how alive my body could feel, especially in a safe environment with someone who loved me. Who knows, it might have given her a new perspective. But at the time I was more concerned about being "the good daughter" and keeping up the pretense of virginity that my father had demanded. I'm not sure if my parents were naive, wanting to believe I was a virgin, or just didn't know how to talk to me about sex.

If they were alive, that is one conversation I'd want to have: What was going through your mind during that time? How has your perspective changed over the years? How did the sexual revolution affect your relationship?

You may not want to talk about sex with your mother, but if you need to, here are a few guidelines to make the conversation easier. The therapists I consulted on this all agreed that because it is such a loaded topic, you must be very clear with yourself about *why* you want to talk to your mother about sex. Are you just curious? Do you think talking about sex will bring you closer? Do you need information from her to understand your own sexuality better? Do you need to resolve past issues? Are you interested in knowing how your body will respond sexually as you age?

Therapist Alexandra Kennedy, M.A., author of *The Infinite Thread*, recommends that you start by writing a letter to your mother or by writing a dialogue about sex between you and your mother, as if you are actually talking with her and she is responding. Because you have the freedom to speak your mind, you are able to go places with your mother that you think would be impossible to explore in person. By writing out your thoughts first, you're also rehearsing your conversation and may find that in your real discussion, you feel safer to discuss certain topics that were otherwise off-limits.

Your mother's comfort is critical here too. Kennedy points out that by telling your mother what you are comfortable and uncomfortable talking about and offering her the same option, you will make it easier for her to open up. Traditionally, mothers—and society at large—have hidden their sexuality from their children, and although you are an adult, you're still your mother's child.

Dr. Marion Solomon, a clinical psychologist and author of *Lean on Me*, suggests that once you have identified your reason, keep in mind your mother's history. Prior to the sexual revolution in the 1960s, mothers were trained not to think or talk about sex. Solomon explains, "If they got involved in anything sexual, it was surreptitiously, and they may not want to divulge that. Those mothers who were involved in the sexual revolution also may not want to talk about what they did. The key is to get your mother started, and to do that you've got to keep out the shame and blame, which is difficult to do because there is usually so much criticism and judgment between mothers and daughters regarding sex." Solomon suggests that you start by asking your mother what she learned from her mother about sex. "To keep her talking, maintain a curious voice tone and respond with phrases such as, 'Tell me more,' 'I never knew that,' and, 'Oh, that's interesting,' rather than 'Why did you do that?' which is sure to shut her down."

Email and letter writing are sometimes an easier way to have this conversation. If you are following the once-a-month format of conversations, you'll already be warmed up and be able to move comfortably into this conversation.

June, Chris's mom, whom we met earlier in the chapter, emailed to Chris her thoughts on her romantic life with Chris's father.

> *Did I tell you that the men in Alaska during World War II got books printed by doctors on "What Makes a Woman Tick?" combining factual knowledge with differences between men and women? I was not too informed, and Audie acted as my teacher. I was curious and wanted to be part of the love that would wash away many of the horrors of war he had been through—twenty-seven months in Alaska and then a long term in Italy during the push as a forward observer in front of the infantry. I could go on with the passionate desires we cultivated and nourished—it took us through the trials and tribulations of Life 101. These memories sustain me today.*

June is obviously comfortable sharing her experiences and has found them to be a comfort to her following the death of her husband. If your mother's husband is still alive, and you want to know more about how to keep sex alive as you age with your husband, follow the lead of Rachel, who talked with her mom, Helen, who is in her sixties, while on vacation.

Rachel, who is in her early forties, with two teenage children, recalls, "We were on vacation, taking a walk, talking about our marriages, when

I asked my mom, 'What's sex like for you now?' We talked about how sex, lovemaking, and passion change, and how they are expressed later in life. She told me that my dad's illness has left him impotent—he's seventy years young—but that hasn't stopped them. She said they've just learned to be more creative in their affection and love for one another."

Having access to our mother's wisdom about sex and her body can be invaluable as we age, especially given our culture's emphasis on youth and reluctance to talk openly about the sexual experiences of older women. Sheila Kitzinger, Ph.D., author of *Woman's Experience of Sex*, writes, "Women themselves, talking about changes in their sexuality as they grow older, often stress that sex is not so 'urgent,' but much more an expression of all that a couple mean to each other." She says that older women who are single are told that they need sex, but then made to feel that geriatric sex is "peculiar, laughable, often disgusting and obscene . . . yet many older women enjoy masturbation and some first discover it after they are widowed."

There are other challenging conversations having to do with intimate relationships that I will address in later conversations about how your parents dealt with conflict and how to talk about issues such as sexual abuse, incest, and being gay.

Now that we've moved through the more difficult aspects of romantic intimacy, it's only fair that we finish this topic with a conversation on the marvelous, miraculous, healing power of romantic love.

Celebrating the Love Between Your Parents

Celebrating the love between your parents by asking your mother to talk about those feelings and memories can be very healing. But do you do it? Most of us have been raised in a social environment that focuses on "ain't it awful." We spend hours analyzing and criticizing what isn't working and become more depressed as a result. We know what hasn't worked; now let's talk about what has worked. Marital therapist John Gottman, Ph.D., in his book *The Seven Principles for Making Marriage Work* (coauthored with Nan Silver), states that 94 percent of the time when couples recall their shared past in a positive light, they are headed for a positive future together as well. Using Gottman's Principle 2—Nurture Your Fondness and Admiration—ask your mother to recall the positive memories with your father or the experiences of romantic love she's had in her life. How did she and your father show their love for each other? What made your mother fall in love with your father? When has your mother felt most appreciated by her husband? What love rituals have they shared between them?

> *Love is a verb.*
> —Anonymous's mother

Kim's mother told her that one of her love rituals is that she always laughs at her husband's jokes no matter how bad they are. Deb writes, "When my father was deployed (while in the navy) my mother would have one of us kids take a picture of her and she'd mail it to Dad. Later in their marriage (I think with the emergence of Marabel Morgan and her book *The Total Woman*) she began to occasionally leave little love notes on the bathroom mirror, on his workbench in the garage, etc." When Chris asked her mother about a love ritual, she was surprised to learn that in forty-five years of marriage, every single time her mother came down the stairs to leave for a social engagement, without fail, her husband whistled at her and said, "I am one lucky guy."

Passing On Her Love Legacy

This topic wouldn't be complete without acknowledging the influence our mothers have had on the romantic love we have experienced in our lives. In the hope that you will be inspired to discover what your mother's love legacy has been to you, I've included comments from several women. Kate, mother of three boys, says her mother taught her the importance of loving and respecting women of all ages. Kate also sends cards to everyone for every occasion to show love, care, and the value of others, which her mother has always done. She laughingly says, "We should own stock in Hallmark." Lynn, a successful entrepreneur, describes a mother whose values were clear. "My mother's love legacy is very strong. She's always told me to enjoy myself, be independent, set expectations that I expect will be met, and be respectful of my husband, especially in public." Kim, a management consultant and stand-up comic, took her mother's love legacy to heart: "If you ain't laughin', why bother?"

Blessed by an Angel

My mother's love legacy centers on appreciation. In the forty-two years that my parents were married, my mother held my father in the highest, most loving light, no matter how difficult he became and no matter how much she complained. As much as I admired her commitment, I was equally incensed with the way I thought she sacrificed herself. I refused to believe that a loving God would want anyone to suffer willingly so that someone else *might* learn to be more compassionate.

A few months after my mother died, I was driving my father home after going out to dinner, when he said out of the blue, "I was such an asshole to your mother. I didn't know what love was until she died. She loved me unconditionally, no matter what I did. Now I know what love is. God, let me show it to my children and grandchildren. Gracie, forgive me." The windows fogged up with the heat of tears. I don't know who was crying more, Dad or me, but I do know that we were blessed by an angel in that moment, and her name was Grace Rose.

When there is great love, there are always miracles.
—WILLA CATHER, in *Quotable Women*
of the Twentieth Century

Activities to Do with Your Mom

❑ Visit the place where your mother and father met or he proposed.

❑ Make a list of all the ways you share love with the special person in your life. Ask your mother to do the same, and compare answers.

❑ Share your romantic fantasies. (Don't freak—I *didn't* say sexual fantasies.)

❑ Have a good laugh, and reread Marabel Morgan's book, *The Total Woman.*

Questions for Your Mom

• Who was your first boyfriend? Who gave you your first kiss?

• What's your favorite memory of falling in love?

• Is there any man you still think about from your early dating years?

• Were you ever engaged to anyone before Dad?

• How did you meet my father? How did he propose? What made you say yes?

• What messages about men did you get from your mother? Your father?

• What's one of the most romantic experiences you've ever had?

• When you see an attractive man, what do you think about?

• What have you enjoyed most about marriage?

• How did you get through the tough times with Dad?

• If you were to meet Dad now, would you still marry him?

• What did you learn after your divorce?

• How did you first learn about sex?

• What's romantic intimacy like for you now?

• What love legacy do you want to leave?

When You Walk Through a Storm

Resolving Conflict

You learned your first lessons on how to get along with people and weather the storms of life from your mother. As early as your terrible twos, you began testing your boundaries with her. In one moment, you were running away when she called you, and in the next moment you were wrapping your arms around her legs like an octopus and refusing to let her go. This dance continued throughout your childhood and adolescence, and if you're really honest with yourself, it still continues today. Push, pull, adjust, push, pull, adjust. For years you've noticed the differences between the two of you—at times sure that the hospital made a mistake and gave you to the wrong mother. But with each passing birthday when you look in the mirror, you begin to notice your mother. She's in your eyes, the curl of your lip, the size of your teeth, or the way you toss your head back when you can't believe what you just saw.

If you get along well with your mom, you enjoy noticing the similarities in the mirror, and they outweigh the differences that annoy you. You look forward to becoming more like your mom. The two of you have learned how to resolve misunderstandings before they turn into a cold war. If you and your mom are out of touch or have a contentious relationship, or you avoid or appease her to get along, those moments with the mirror—and her—can be painful.

Mother-daughter relationships have their tense moments and difficult times, and they are unlikely to disappear completely. But when you disagree, you can lessen the pain and resentment that you feel by learning how to do with your mother what my friend Sam Horn suggests in her book, *Tongue Fu*—ask yourself, "How would I feel if I were in her situation?" Talking with your mother about how the two of you have responded when you're under stress and what you've done that has helped you through difficult times can help lessen the tension. This type of talk is a lot more interesting and supportive than rehashing old issues that never change and trying to change one another.

Here are four areas that we'll look at to help you create a more supportive environment for "fair fighting" with your mother.

- Finding out more about your mother's experience of conflict in her life
- How the two of you can resolve old issues that may still be bothering one or both of you
- How your mother has handled difficult life transitions
- How to deal with a difficult mother, including specific words to use when she responds in angry, hurtful, or inappropriate ways

Conflict Is Part of the Human Condition

Conflict, while rarely pleasant, is part of the human condition. Every culture, every community, every family, and every person has conflict somewhere in their lives. Conflict is involved even when you are making a decision about what will make you happy. Do I go for a walk, or do I read a book? All choices—between two ideas, beliefs, experiences, people, and situations—involve conflict. Where we get into trouble with conflict is when we see it as wrong or bad. If we held the belief that conflict is normal and decided that we would learn how to respond more effectively to it, it wouldn't have to be so frightening or irritating or divisive. Having many ways of looking at a situation can actually be desirable, because it allows for a more holistic solution that involves everyone affected by the decision. Our challenge is learning how to be more comfortable with conflict. Instead of fighting or fleeing or freezing in response to conflict, let's learn to flow with it.

I experienced my father as dictatorial and my mother as agreeable and passive with him. Mom rarely got angry or raised her voice. Tears were the way she expressed her frustrations. When Dad and I butted heads, I learned there was only one option with him, and it was his option, his way. Resolving conflict for me has always been a challenge because I never learned good negotiating skills. I was surprised to learn in my early forties when I began to study conflict resolution that it's okay for people around me to get angry. People do get mad, I heard. As long as they don't verbally or physically abuse me, I can now respond assertively instead of aggressively, passively, or passive-aggressively to their anger (most of the time). What a concept!

As you begin to negotiate the world of conflict more successfully, the first thing you'll want to do is identify what you're feeling and what your feelings are trying to tell you before you express yourself to your mother (or any other person). So often when we're upset, we lash out at Mom or go into hiding, and never take the time to explore what is really going on in our mind and heart. All we know is we feel strongly about something and, dammit, we're mad (or sad, scared, guilty, ashamed, confused, . . .) and *it's all her fault!* And we're going to let her have it or complain about her to someone else.

*Anger is a lot like a piece of shredded wheat caught under
your dentures. If you leave it there you'll get a blister, and you
gotta eat Jell-O all week. If you get rid of it, the sore heals and
you feel better.*
—SOPHIA ("MA"), in *The Golden Girls*

In our society (and most other societies for that matter), women have been raised to believe that certain feelings are good and right and others are bad and wrong. Happy is good, anger is bad. We're not taught that all types of feelings are a normal part of being human. Feelings have a powerful purpose that can be used to help us resolve conflict. Feelings are road signs that tell you where to turn next.

Think of a recent misunderstanding or disagreement with your mother. From the list in the following box, identify what you were feeling. Then read across the list and listen to what your emotions are trying to tell you.

What Are Your Emotions Trying to Tell You?

Anger, frustration, annoyance	I don't like this. Change it now!
Hurt (emotional)	I'm in pain. I ache. Soothe me.
Sadness, disappointment	I've experienced a loss. Help me let go. Fill me with something new.
Fear, worry, doubt	I'm in danger. Protect me [from real or imagined danger].
Guilt	I've gone against my values [or the values of someone else who is important to me]. Make it right.
Shame	I feel unworthy. Help me feel valuable.
Confusion	I don't know what to do. Help me get clear.
Longing	I really want this. Please get it for me.
Excitement	Something great has happened to me. I am anticipating something really good. Show me enthusiasm. Jump for joy. Share it.
Happiness	I like this. Give me more.
Gratitude	I am blessed. Appreciate the moment.

Once you know what you're feeling when you're upset and what your heart (emotional center) is trying to tell you, you can take better care of yourself and respond more effectively to your mother.

To become clearer about your own issues with your mother and to know yourself better, I encourage you to finish the sentence completions about how you are feeling. Use either the same misunderstanding from the previous exercise, or choose another one as you respond. Often simply acknowledging your feelings to yourself before you talk with your mother will make it easier to talk when you do get together. You'll notice that the statements move from negative to positive. This is done purposely so that you express the full range of feelings and not get stuck in just the negative. Answer them quickly in one sentence to access your first thoughts.

How Are You Feeling?

I'm angry about . . .   *I am willing to . . .*
I'm sad about . . .   *I'm inspired by . . .*
I'm scared of . . .   *I'm excited about . . .*
I need . . .   *I'm happy about . . .*
I would like you to . . .   *I'm grateful for . . .*
I'm sorry that . . .   *I forgive you for . . .*

This exercise can be very cathartic. Some women have found it helpful to read their responses to their mother—and to invite their mother to do the same—as a way to know more about each other. If you choose to do this with your mother, here are points to keep in mind.

- When you listen to each other's answers, the response is simply, "Thank you." This is not the time to discuss your reaction. It's time simply to acknowledge each other. You can go back and discuss your reactions after you've had time to think things over.
- Alternate your responses. You read one; your mother reads one.
- You don't have to have all the answers, and some days you won't be experiencing some of these feelings. But don't use that as an excuse to avoid being honest with yourself or your mother. This is a great way to become more aware of yourself and your mother and let each other in on what's happening in your lives.

With practice (I recommend doing this at least once a week by yourself, preferably once a day until you're able to recognize your emotions quickly) you'll find yourself feeling more lighthearted; instead of ignoring or suppressing your feelings, you're getting them out of your system and moving on.

How Do You and Your Mother Handle Differences?

Once you know what you're feeling and before you talk with your mom, think back to past conflicts with her and ask yourself if you are a conflict avoider, conflict confronter, or conflict resolver:

- *Conflict avoider:* Doesn't speak up, withdraws, distracts, cries, sighs, rolls eyes and walks away, blames others, passively manipulates.
- *Conflict confronter:* Yells, demands, points, belittles, criticizes, invades others' space, swears, threatens, blames others, aggressively manipulates.
- *Conflict resolver:* Speaks calmly and firmly, invites questions, asks questions, acknowledges differences, seeks to understand and get agreement.

How would you describe your mother when she is with you? Knowing what conflict style you and your mother are with each other will help you break old patterns that haven't given you the results you want. While it may seem doable only in books, your goal is to be a conflict resolver. It is possible.

I Love You, I Believe In You, I Will Protect You

I was a conflict confronter with my mother, who was a classic conflict avoider. When anyone took my mom to task, especially my father, she'd listen until the person was finished and then retreat to the bedroom where she usually took a nap, cried, took a pill, or, I imagine, ate from her secret Hershey's almond bar cache in her lingerie drawer. I don't ever remember her challenging others' decisions or criticisms, at least in my presence, except once.

When I was in the seventh grade, I was taken into a school hallway during the middle of the school day by my nun teacher, slapped across the face repeatedly, and pushed down the stairs for "speaking blasphemously." (I had sworn a friend to secrecy about a confidential family matter. She told her mother, who called the principal and told her that I was not to associate with her daughter. The principal told my teacher to handle it.) Humiliated, I ran out of school and all the way home. When my mother opened the front door, I burst into tears and told her what happened. She hugged me, told me that no one had a right to hurt me, and said she would handle it. She grabbed her coat, took my hand, and walked me back to the principal's office. She firmly demanded an apology from the principal and my teacher and a guarantee that no hand would ever touch me again. Having accomplished her mission, she took me out of school for the rest of the day and walked me home again, holding my hand the entire way. When we arrived at the house, she went into her bedroom. A few minutes later, she called me in, pulled out two Hershey's chocolate almond bars from her cache, and smiled as she handed me my own bar. My mother's Hershey's bar ritual said it all. "Some days are better than others. I love you, I believe in you, I will protect you." All was right with the world again. Her response was one of the most loving and bravest memories I have of her.

In the final months of my mother's life, I mentioned that Hershey's bar episode to her and told her how proud I was of her that afternoon.

"You know what was best about that?" I asked her.

She laughed and said, "The end of it?"

"You believed in me and stood up for me."

Mom got very quiet and began to cry, saying, "I tried my best to be a good mother, and I often felt I disappointed you."

I could hear the pain in her voice. I didn't know what to say, so I just lay down in her hospital bed with her, held her hand, and hugged her. As I left the house that night, I was glad I'd taken the time to recall that story and tell her how I felt. However, if I could do the conversation over, I would have also asked her, "What other difficult situations have you been proud of the way you handled?" so that she would have had an opportunity to share some of her best moments with me. I would also have brought her a Hershey's bar.

We can all dredge up painful issues that we've gone around and around on with no resolution. But what does it serve to keep bringing them up except to make us feel bad all over again? The times I sat in righteous judgment of my mother never encouraged her or helped her to be stronger. If anything, they demoralized her and kept her stuck. What helped her was when I reminded her of her strength and belief in doing the right thing for herself and her family.

What positive, healing, or inspiring memories do you have of your mother's responding to conflict with you? If you draw a blank, think of your family or her friends or parents. Look for something positive. Write your memories and what you've learned about how to handle conflict in your journal now. Once you've finished this chapter, you'll be ready to share your insights with your mother.

Revisiting Old Conflicts

If it is necessary to revisit an old conflict to find resolution, take the time to think through your alternatives before you speak with your mom. If you have a tendency to lose your train of thought, go blank, or explode, script out your initial comments and ask a friend to role-play them with you. If you find yourself in the middle of a disagreement and don't know how to resolve it, take a break, even if it's just for a few minutes to calm down. And if you're still getting nowhere, ask yourself if there is some piece of truth that one of you is withholding from the other that needs to be expressed.

Natalie, a mother of two and a director of a nonprofit neighborhood association, and her mother, Jessica, are both conflict confronters. During a day trip to visit relatives, Jessica was describing a conversation she overheard between a group of women, one of whom she mentioned was black (Jessica and Natalie are caucasian). Natalie, who admits to correcting her mother's language when she feels it's inappropriate, interrupted Jessica and said, "Did you need to tell me that one woman was black?"

Jessica exploded and said, "I can't talk to you. Nothing I ever say is right. I have to walk on eggshells whenever we're together."

Natalie shouted back, "You wouldn't have said that if they were all white women."

"It doesn't make a difference. You make it sound like I'm prejudiced. I'm not prejudiced," Jessica yelled defensively.

"Mom, that's easy for you to say, but you sound prejudiced when you say that. If a person of color was standing here and you said exactly what you just said, that person would feel tension. I just want you to be sensitive to other people's experience, not just your own."

There was stony silence in the car. Natalie knew her mother wouldn't make the first move. She also knew it was going to be a very long trip if she didn't find some way to reconnect with her mother. As she reflected on their heated exchange, she had a flash of insight about why she was so angry with her mother. She had never explained to her mother why her mother's comments were such a hot button for her and why she's so sensitive to racial issues.

When Natalie was growing up, her parents employed an African American housekeeper named Bertha who cooked and cleaned to the point of exhaustion. Natalie felt she was poorly treated and overworked by her mother. Natalie began to cry as she explained why she held her mother to such a high standard and acknowledged that it had a lot to do with the way Jessica had treated Bertha.

Natalie recalls, "My mom admitted how bad she felt and how wrong was done there. It was amazing how quickly all my anger toward her evaporated because of that one simple act of her acknowledging her mistreatment of Bertha. What was even more surprising was how my mother responded to my truth quickly and remorsefully. We decided to make agreements with each other. She agreed to pay more attention to her language and watch what she said, and I agreed that I would be more understanding and wouldn't jump on her all the time. We've had disagreements since then, but now we're much more honest with each other, and instead of yelling and blaming each other, we can talk things through with respect."

Agree to Disagree

Dialogue is so very important during conflict, and it's usually the first thing to disappear when conflict arises. If you find you absolutely cannot resolve an issue, be willing to agree to disagree. This simple decision will reduce tension and allow both of you some time to think through what you want to do next. If this doesn't work, suggest a time-out, but also make sure you agree to check in with each other at an agreed-on time—twenty-four hours, a day, a week later—to see if there's been any shift in either of your perspectives and to keep the door open. Too many times I've heard of mothers and daughters who had an argument where one walked off in a huff and neither called to check on each other because they were so angry. Days turned into months into years, with both women aching inside and too proud to be the first one to reach out, often only when crisis arose, as was the case with Dawn and her mother, Pam.

Dawn, now in her early thirties, was seventeen when she stopped talking to her mother. "My mother was very critical of all her children, constantly demeaning us in front of each other and friends. None of us seven children ever stood up to her because we were taught to respect our elders. I thought I'd learned to shut out her negativity, but it finally got to me the night of my first high school prom. I was seventeen. When I came down the stairs to meet my boyfriend, my mother said, 'You look like a slut. Go wash your face. You will not go out of the house looking like that.' I was so angry I didn't come home that night, and the next day I moved out and never looked back. I lived with my boyfriend's family, graduated from high school, got a job, got married, and moved across the country."

Ten years later, when Dawn was in the middle of a baby shower for her first child, her sister called her: "Mom's had a stroke and lost her ability to talk. She may not make it." Dawn was on the next plane home and went immediately to the hospital. She recalled, "It had been ten years since I'd talked to my mom. I prayed that if she lived, I would never let an argument separate us again. It took my mother a whole year to learn to speak again. She finally apologized for what happened. I had already forgiven her." Dawn remarks with surprise, "I often think of the irony of the situation: my mother's words drove me away, and my mother's lack of words brought me back. I wouldn't have called her if this hadn't happened. What a mistake that would have been."

If your disagreement is so intense that you're at a stalemate, before you completely cut yourself off from your mother, do what you can to suggest the two of you see a therapist together for one session, and preferably three to six sessions, to find a way to deal more effectively with each other.

I Understand How That Hurt You, and I'm Sorry

Stella Resnick, psychologist and author of *The Pleasure Zone*, reminds women who have unresolved issues from the past with their mothers that the woman you talk to today is different from the woman who did what she did in the past. Don't assume that she still harbors the same feelings she did previously. Like Natalie's and Dawn's mothers, your mother may regret what she did but not be able to bring herself to apologize for fear of losing face and your love. Resnick suggests that if your mother doesn't understand that saying "I'm sorry" to you will clear the air and allow you to let go of the past, tell her so. If she still doesn't respond, Resnick explains, "You have to be the bigger person. You can remind yourself that you know something your mother doesn't know about forgiveness, which can actually give you more compassion for your mother and make it easier for you to move on."

Empathize, Apologize, and Forgive

Resnick says it is important to know your goal—and the goal is *not* to hang your mother. Your goal is to create some sort of resolution that involves letting go of the past. She offers a three-step plan for forgiveness: empathize, apologize, and forgive. You want to spell out to your mother what was so painful without trying to make her feel guilty and forever bear the burden of her past sins. You want to give her an out.

Daughter: Mom, I'd like to tell you what you did that offended me. Are you open to hearing it?

Hopefully, your mother says yes. If she doesn't, you must do your own healing work. If she does say yes, your response could be:

Daughter: When you criticized me for taking that promotion and not being a good mother, that really hurt me. I'd like to know if you regret what you said and, if you do, to apologize. It would really help me let this go. If you still feel the same way, there's nothing I can do about it, except tell you that I did the best I could and I could really use your support.

What we want to hear our mother say is, "I understand how that hurt you, and I'm sorry." We want empathy. And then we want our mother to say, "Please forgive me. I made a mistake." And then we want to be able to forgive her. Otherwise, Resnick says, "this exercise is pointless. This is not about beating up on your mother. It's about healing with your mother."

When the situation is reversed, and you're the one who has hurt your mother's feelings, reverse the process.

Daughter: Mom, I want to apologize for embarrassing you in front of your friends by saying that you didn't know what you were talking about the other night. I'm guessing you must have been pretty embarrassed. I'm wondering how you're feeling about that now?

After your mother has expressed her feelings and assuming she said it still hurts or continues to have a negative impact on her, your response could be:

Daughter: I understand how much that hurt you, and I'm sorry. Please forgive me; I made a mistake."

If you're unable to let go of a painful conflict or hurt from the past, Resnick says that after going through this forgiveness process with no resolution, it's time to stop talking about it with your mother and do the work on your own with a therapist.

We Teach People How to Treat Us

When you anticipate or get into a difficult conversation with your mother, think of her as a friend or coworker whom you respect. What you're doing is retraining your mind to see her differently. There is a saying, "We teach people how to treat us," which in this case means that if your mother mistreats you, however you respond to her is teaching her how to respond back to you. If your mother criticizes you and you say nothing in response while continuing to interact with her, you are telling her that it is okay for her to criticize you. If you blow up at her while yelling, "You can't treat me like that," and she walks off in a huff, you've taught her that any time she gives you feedback or advice (her definition of criticism), the interaction will be extremely unpleasant, and she'll disengage. I'm not advocating tolerating anyone's criticism or not speaking your mind; I'm suggesting that you look at how you and your mother interact during conflict so you can make it easier on yourself regardless of what she chooses to do.

If you haven't been able to resolve an issue, review the following suggestions, and experiment with one or a combination in your next conversation with your mother:

- Picture your mother as a friend or colleague whom you respect and who is having a difficult day.
- Use different words. Change the word *but* to the word *and* ("I know you don't want to talk about this, *and* [not *but*] it's important to me that we do.").
- Use a different tone of voice. Lower your voice and speak more calmly.
- Tell how you would feel in her circumstance, and ask her how she feels. Don't define her feeling. Rather than say, "Mom, you are really upset," say, "Mom, I'd be really upset if I were you. How are you feeling?"
- If you tend to talk a lot, be more succinct and listen more.
- If you are usually quiet, speak up more often and state your opinion.
- Have the conversation in a different location or during a different time of day.
- Shift from complaint to exploration. Explain your problem briefly, and then ask your mother for her own personal experience.
- Offer how you may have contributed to the problem.

The past is history, the future is a mystery, this moment is a gift. That is why they call it "the present."

—Anonymous

"I Never Thought You Needed Me"

Sheila Heen writes in *Difficult Conversations: How to Discuss What Matters Most*, that stating how you contributed to the problem will melt anger and keep the conversation flowing. It may be awkward, embarrassing, or even painful to admit, but the results can be dramatic and may significantly shorten the amount of time you spend reaching an agreement or putting the hurt or disappointment behind the two of you.

The technique of stating your contribution to the problem is best used when you or your mother, or both of you, are reserved and have difficulty being vulnerable and expressing real feelings. Your openness can set the stage for her to reveal more of herself. Be careful, though: this technique can backfire if you're the one who always takes the blame for what happens between you and your mother. You'll end up feeling like a victim again, and your mother will not have the opportunity to take responsibility for her actions.

Tevyan, an animal lover who lives on a Texas ranch with her husband and daughter, was very close to her father, who died of cancer when she was fourteen. She explains, "I was the youngest of seven children. My daddy took me to school every day. At the end of the school day, the bus would drop me off at his workplace. I'd play or do my homework sitting in a chair right next to him until he finished his day, and then we'd drive home together. Mom was always busy with the other kids, especially my sister, Cindi, who was always sick as a child. After Daddy died, my mother and I were in our own little worlds, and we didn't talk much. Then I got married at age sixteen, mostly to get more attention and affection, and my mother and I drifted even further apart. I felt bad, but not bad enough to do anything about our distance."

Tevyan remembers the moment everything changed. "My sister,

Cindi, was diagnosed with breast cancer and died three years ago at age twenty-eight. She was only ten months older than me, and we were best friends. I was there with her from the moment she was diagnosed until the end, which helped my mom finally see me as a person, not just her baby daughter who was distant and uncaring."

After Cindi's death, Tevyan's mother went into a serious depression, became critically ill, and slowly began giving up her will to live. During a particularly trying moment with her mother, Tevyan burst out, "Oh this is great! Daddy died. Cindi died. And now you're going to die too. I need you Mom."

Tevyan's willingness to be vulnerable, one of her greatest fears, became her greatest asset when she shared it with her mother. Her mother began to cry, saying, "I never thought of you as needing me."

Tevyan's next comment of admitting her own mistake is one of the most powerful statements anyone can make in the midst of conflict (unless you chronically take the blame in order to pacify your mother). Tevyan explained, "I guess part of the distance between us is my fault because I never relied on you; I always had Daddy and my brothers. We'll get through this as a family. Nobody's giving up."

"Tevyan, I love you."

That was the turning point for Tevyan and her mother. Tevyan remarked, "That was the first time in my entire life my mother said, 'I love you.' Now she'll tell me 'I love you, I miss you, I need you.' There's not a day that goes by that I don't talk to her. Sometimes we talk now for upwards of an hour. She's had five heart attacks and so much cancer, and yet she keeps surprising her doctors and me. Even though we live twenty miles apart, I try to see her every day. I don't know how much longer she'll be with us, but we're doing everything we can to enjoy the time she has left."

Be Assertive in Your Responses

There are many roads to dealing successfully with conflict and distance in your relationship with your mother. If you're still not sure what to say or how to approach her, read through the following list of sixteen specific responses your mother could give you and what you can say back to her to keep communication flowing. (There are four more response/answers in the next chapter on secrets.)

If you find yourself resisting the suggested dialogue, feeling that it's too aggressive or unemotional or not the way you speak with your mother, give it a try anyway. Change takes time. Practicing these statements out loud, at least ten times (preferably until you know them by heart), with a friend or to yourself in the mirror, can genuinely help you feel more comfortable with them. Play around with the words if they feel awkward to you, but know that the more often you hear yourself say them out loud, the more likely these statements will feel like your own.

Mother: That is a dead issue.

Daughter: Mom, it may be a dead issue for you, and [not *but*] it's not for me. Would you please give me five more minutes, and then if we still haven't cleared things up, I'll take a break and we can decide what to do later. I've brought a timer with me so that you know I'm serious about adhering to five minutes. [This might get a laugh and lighten things up somewhat.]

Mother: You're making that up.

Daughter: Mom, I know you think I'm making this up, and [not *but*] I can see why you might think that, and [not *but*] this is how I see things right now. Maybe if you told me again why you think I'm making this up, I'll better understand your perspective.

Mother: That's not the way it was.

Daughter: Mother, it seems we see things very differently and that's okay. It's more important to me that we understand each other. Let's talk to [Eileen] and [Jeanne] about this and see what they remember. Maybe they can help us get to the essence of the situation.

Mother: I don't know.
Daughter: Mom, if you did know, what do you think the answer
             would be? [Watch your voice tone here. Keep it neutral,
             not sarcastic.]

Mother: Don't be ridiculous.
Daughter: Mother, this may seem ridiculous to you, and [not *but*] it's
             not to me. Please humor me, and let's stay with this for
             just a little while longer.

Mother: Why are you hurting me like this?
Daughter: Mom, I hear that you think I'm hurting you and that must
             feel terrible. [Pause just long enough for her to nod yes.] If
             you'll give me a few minutes to explain, I think you'll see
             that I'm trying to help you and why your answer to this
             question is so important to me.

There may be times when your mother doesn't know how to respond to your questions and acts in a childish manner. If your mother
acts like a child, love the child in her and speak to the adult. Thinking through all her possible reactions will make it easier for you
to reply lovingly and firmly and continue with the conversation. Review the following situations for healthy responses to rebellious behavior.

She Won't Stop Talking
Daughter: Mom, it sounds as if you've got a lot more to say about this.
             Let's stop for right now and allow me to give you this jour-
             nal [or tape recorder] to write [or record] more of your
             thoughts.

She Contradicts Herself
Keep notes. Be specific and compassionate. Memory is selective, especially when you're in the hot seat. Decide if it's really important that
your mother be accurate at all times. If not, let it go. If it is important to
you, tell her how you feel, and offer to help her find the truth.

Daughter: Mom, I'm confused. The last time we spoke about this, I remember you saying that I could have great-grandma's antique hat. Now you're saying that you gave it to Jeanne because she asked for it. What made you change your mind?

Or:

Mom, I remember you telling me a few years ago that I could have great-grandma's antique hat. I am feeling really disappointed that you forgot about me and gave it to Jeanne instead. In the future, before you give any family heirlooms away, I'd really appreciate it if you'd talk with all of us children about it first. Would you do that for me?

She Cries

Some mothers use crying or tears as a way to distract you and themselves from the issue at hand. While I don't suggest that you always force your mother to continue talking, sometimes she may need your support and encouragement to get beyond her fear or pain. Only you and your mother will know if it's better to take a break.

Daughter: Mom, this seems very upsetting to you. Let me get you some tissues, and see if you can talk through your tears. What you're saying is very important to me, and I want to hear your thoughts.

Or:

Mom, let me get you some tissues. Let's take a break and come back to this in fifteen minutes.

She Laughs at Everything You Say

Daughter: Mom, I know you think this is funny, but it's not funny to me. I'd like you to be more serious, or tell me what I can do to help you take me more seriously.

She Storms Out of the Room or Explodes

If you know your mother tends to walk away or explode when a situation gets uncomfortable, realize that it may be her way of controlling the situation. Agree ahead of time what course you'll take if your discussion gets out of hand.

Daughter: Mom, I have some things I'd like to talk to you about that may make both of us angry. I'd like to find a way to keep you focused on talking with me instead of walking out of the room [or exploding] if you get upset. Would you be willing to stay with me and work it out? If not, then I'd like to suggest that we find a counselor together so that we can find peace with this issue.

You Explode

Daughter: Mom, I'm feeling so mad right now. I'm sorry I blew up. I'm going to take a walk around the block, and then I'll be back so we can decide what to do next.

She Starts to Criticize You

If your mother criticizes you, first let her finish. Unless she is verbally abusing you, letting her vent will end her tirade sooner than if you lash back or run away. Take a deep breath, and ask yourself if the criticism is valid. If what she's saying isn't valid, here are three choices to consider:

- Say nothing, pause a second, and then change the subject. A sincere compliment, unrelated to the issue you're discussing, will distract her temporarily and move you out of the spotlight—for example: "Mom, you did such a great job on that project for church."
- Say, "I'll choose to ignore that, Mom."
- Say, "Mom, it sounds as if you're criticizing me. Is that what you wanted to do?"

If the criticism is valid and you just don't want to hear it, it is in your best interests to acknowledge your mother's insight and ask her to give you feedback in a more loving way the next time.

Daughter: Mom, I appreciate your feedback. You may be right. [This is a very powerful statement that allows you to acknowledge her without agreeing with her.] Next time when you have something to tell me that you think will make me a better person, it would be more helpful if you would say it in a more loving way.

If your mother is verbally abusive, take control. A critical person will continue to attack you if you don't stop him or her. Acknowledge the violation immediately. By ignoring what your mother says, you'll only be subjected to more negative comments. Maintain a calm voice. Sounding whiny or angry won't work, because, in effect, you're feeding your mother's negative behavior.

Daughter: Mom, when you tell me what's wrong with me, I feel really angry. I'm an adult. In the future, please give me advice only when I ask for it. Now, we were talking about how you handled money when you were my age . . .

She Won't Return Your Call

Write your mother a letter, letting her know how important she is to you and that when she's ready to talk, you'll be there for her:

Dear Mom,
I'm feeling really sad and disappointed that you've chosen not to respond to my interest in your life. If and when you decide that you'd like to tell me more, I'm here for you. I love you.

Stay open to her and keep loving yourself.

The Two of You Don't Agree

You don't have to agree with your mother! Yes, we've been socialized to believe that if we don't agree, we're bad daughters. We are forever destined to feel guilty or anxious about this. Let this go. Virginia Satir, the world-renowned family therapist, said, "We learn to love through our similarities and we learn to grow through our differences." Use your disagreement to understand your mother and yourself better.

Daughter: Mom, I feel differently than you do about this. While I wish we felt the same way, it's more important to me that

I understand you than agree with you. So, if you're willing, I'd like to hear more about how you came to this decision.

The Two of You Can't Seem to Resolve Your Differences

If you differ about an issue that is critical to you, then you might choose to find a therapist to help you work through the dilemma on your own, or ask your mother to see a family therapist with you.

If control is an issue, and one or both of you have a driving need to be right, ask yourself if it's more important to be right or to be loving in this particular situation. A phrase that helped me through difficult times was, "If I knew we would never see each other again, would this still be important to resolve?" If it is, stay with the issue and get help. If it's not, try the words of author Stephen Covey, "Let's just agree to disagree."

Daughter: Mom, I can see this is important to both of us, and [not *but*] right now, it's not important enough for me to keep arguing about. I love you and want to find a way through this. How about if we agree and find other things that we can spend time talking about. [Saying this in a firm and kind voice tone, as a statement rather than a question, will help guide your mother in a more conciliatory direction.]

Forgiveness is giving up all hopes for a better past.
—DIANE CIRINCIONE (author of *Love Is Letting Go of Fear*), from a 1990 speech

Practicing Ahead of Time Will Keep You on Track

Preparation and practice are two of the major keys to learning new ways of thinking, feeling, and acting. If you find yourself reverting to old behavior, read this chapter again and keep in mind the words of C. Leslie Charles, author of *Why Is Everyone So Cranky?* "I've learned that self-improvement comes through exploration, acknowledgment, and acceptance: the ability to say, 'Yes, I do this, and now that I've admitted it, I can change this behavior.' "

Making amends with your mother can be one of the most satisfying and important things you do in life. Learning how to accept your differences and embrace your similarities are skills you can learn. More simply, it's a decision. It doesn't mean things will be perfect, and it doesn't mean you'll have a perfect mother or be the perfect daughter. But it does mean that you will find your mother and yourself easier to be with, and when you look in the mirror, you'll like what you see.

> *Give to others what you want to receive—love, support, appreciation, healing, and acknowledgment—and you will get it back. . . . Healing others is not just a gift you are giving the world. It is also a gift to yourself.*
> —SANAYA ROMAN, *Personal Power Through Awareness*

Activities to Do with Your Mom

❑ Perform a forgiveness ritual by writing down what you're both angry about and burning the paper in a private ritual.
❑ Write each other an "I'm sorry" letter.
❑ Work with a family therapist.
❑ Make a list of the times you've successfully worked through differences and what you did to resolve the problem.

Questions for Your Mom

- How did you and your mother deal with your differences?
- Did Grandma and her mother get along? Why (or why not)?
- How was conflict handled between your parents? Your siblings?
- Did anyone in your family ever stop speaking to each other? What was the cause? How long did the silence last?
- Who is one of the most difficult persons you've ever had to interact with? What made this person difficult? How did you handle the situation?
- What's one of the most difficult or trying times you've gone through

in your life? How did it turn out? What could you have done differently? When you look back on it now, what did you learn that has helped you become a better person?

- What memories, independent of me, bubble up when you recall past anger and conflict that is still unresolved for you? That you resolved?
- Is there anything I've done that you haven't been able to forgive me for? Could we work on it now?
- Who is one of the easiest persons you've ever gotten along with? What made it easy to talk to that person? Did you ever have disagreements? How did you work them out?
- When have you felt strong and proud of yourself for getting through a difficult time?

Do You Want to Know a Secret?

Family Secrets

Our earliest experiences of secrets begin in childhood. You overhear your mother on the phone whispering to the caller, "Of course, I can keep a secret." When you ask her to explain, she says, "It's a surprise." As adolescents, we discover that a secret shared with a girlfriend today often becomes everyone's business tomorrow. By the time we're adult women, we've been around the block and are more careful. We choose our confidantes wisely. And when we find those few friends with whom we can share our joys and sorrows, successes and failures, and trust we will be accepted, we count our blessings. Our mothers may or may not be in this meaningful and charmed circle of intimacy. We hesitate to speak our truth to her if there's a chance she might be disappointed in us or won't approve. Our mothers keep secrets from us to protect us and maintain our respect. We both hold back, afraid of losing love or control, only to find out that once the truth is shared, painful as it may initially be, there is relief. When we share the deepest, darkest parts of ourselves with each other, we become more authentic. We experience a deeper sense of belonging, of being known and being accepted for who we are.

My mother couldn't keep a secret if her life depended on it. At least that was what I thought while growing up. From her revelations about herself and gossip about family and neighbors to the whispered reminders of what to hide from my father (new clothes, new ideas, or my new boyfriend), my mother bared her soul to me.

I thought she told me everything until the day I told her I was leaving my marriage. It was 1979. I was twenty-seven. She was fifty-nine. I asked her if she'd ever been attracted to other men besides my father.

"I'll tell you a secret," she said, "if you promise not to . . ."

"Tell anyone," I laughed, not prepared for what was to follow.

"After Mother died, I was having a hard time. Do you remember when I went to visit your grandfather down in Florida?"

I counted back sixteen years. It was 1964. I was eleven at the time. She was forty-four and was gone a month—the first time she'd ever been away from us children and my father. I remembered writing her "I-miss-you-when-are-you-coming-home" letters.

She interrupted my musing and continued, "On the flight down, I met a man who became quite taken with me and wanted me to meet him at a hotel when we got off the plane. I was flattered but declined. He was very handsome and very nice to me. He was also very persistent, writing his home phone number down on a business card and folding it into my hand. I imagined myself running away with him. He said that if I changed my mind at any time, he would be waiting. In the month I was in Florida, I actually picked up the phone a few times because I was so unhappy with your father. But I decided not to, because as difficult as your father is, I loved him and still do. But what was even more important was that I loved you children too much to leave you without a mother."

I sat in front of her dumbfounded. My mind whirled with so many thoughts and feelings. First I thought about her. Did she still think about this man? Did she regret her decision? Once I got past how she felt, I wondered about our family. What if she had left? What if I'd never seen her again? What would our lives have been like? And then I wondered why she told me. Did she think I should stay in my marriage? Did she think I should leave?

I never asked these questions, and we never talked about it again. I was so uncomfortable with her revelation, particularly because my marriage was ending, that I changed the subject that day and never went back to it. I wish I had had the knowledge and skill then that I have today, because I know now there was a lot more to my mother than I ever guessed. Had I known the right questions to ask and how to approach her, who knows how much stronger our relationship could have been in the remaining eleven years she lived and the paths we might have taken?

What Do You Consider a Secret?

Secrets told and untold have the power to change lives, which is what makes them both alluring and frightening. Secrets come in all shapes and sizes, with family secrets being one of the most stressful on mothers and daughters. Family secrets include, but are not limited to, withholding information about health problems, incest, infidelity, and addictions. There are also personal secrets, which include new choices, sexual preference, prejudices, and frozen evaluations of people and situations from the past.

The secrets we'll be focusing on in this chapter are family secrets, past and present, that need to be revisited because they're still bothering you or because they could affect you or your mother's future, and personal disclosure, which will help both of you understand each other better.

We have more words to describe the nuances of how we
deceive each other than to describe how we love.
—HARRIET LERNER, *The Dance of Deception*

Donna, a busy, single, working mother in her forties, laughs when she says, "Growing up, my mother and I could never keep a secret from each other. Even after I moved out and lived 400 miles away, she still couldn't resist telling me at Thanksgiving what would be underneath the tree for me at Christmas. Now I realize how much she didn't tell me—and still doesn't unless I ask. The big stuff—her health, my father's alcoholism, her fear about aging—usually sits quietly under the dining room table at holiday meals until we're doing the evening dishes and I start asking questions. Even then, it's still not easy to get her to talk."

It's important to remember that our mothers were raised in a time when most personal issues were not talked about, especially with one's children, whether that child was four or forty. Women have changed and rules have changed, but that doesn't mean our mothers' attitudes have changed. Nor does it mean that we are comfortable asking our mother to open the door to her closet or disclose the contents of our own. But if we want things to change for the better, it is up to us to lead the way.

While I don't pretend you'll find this an easy topic to talk about with your mother, there will be rewards for approaching the subject—even if your mother has no secrets from you or is unwilling to talk about a secret. You will show your mother and yourself that you are serious about cleaning up messy memories, and you'll be one step closer to letting go of what you can't control and acting on what you can control.

How Do You Know What Secrets Are Appropriate to Tell and to Ask About?

In my interpersonal communication programs, I tell my audiences that there are five topics to avoid as small talk if you want to create quick rapport with someone: sex, politics, religion, money, and personal issues such as health and divorce. It doesn't seem to matter if the person you're talking with is your boss, a *60 Minutes* reporter, or your mother; differing opinions about these loaded issues are sure to create tension. Add a secret into the equation, and you have a story for the *National Enquirer*. No wonder we don't want to talk to our mothers about our private thoughts, choices, and behaviors. Yet all of these topics, when discussed with your mother at the right time, offer an incredible opportunity to create more understanding and intimacy between the two of you.

So you're wondering if I'm telling you to bare all to your mother? No. Not all secrets need to or should be told. What's important is to distinguish between what is a private matter and what is a secret. Privacy allows for healthy boundaries and maintains our individuality. Dr. Harriet Lerner points out in *The Dance of Deception* that knowing the difference between privacy and secrecy is very important. Private matters do not affect another person's choices. Secrecy is hiding something from another person that would affect that person's choices. Most family secrets fall into the latter category and destroy trust, lower self-esteem, and distance family members from each other.

> *I am in perfect health, and hear it said I look better than ever*
> *I did in my life, which is one of those lies one is always glad*
> *to hear.*
>
> —LADY MARY WORTLEY MONTAGU,
> *The Best Letters of Lady*
> *Mary Wortley Montagu*

What Secrets Might Your Mother Be Withholding from You?

It never occurred to me that my mother withheld anything from me until I realized that she'd kept her Florida fantasy from me for sixteen years—not that I would have expected her to tell me at age eleven that she considered leaving my father, but that she might never have told me her secret unless I'd asked the question. Was her disclosure critical to my future? No. Did her disclosure affect our relationship in a positive way? Yes. She became more real to me, which deepened my respect for her and opened the door to more honest communication.

Keeping my mother's secret in the back of my mind, I became curious when women told me, "My mother and I have no secrets between us," or "We tell each other everything." When I followed up with the question, "How do you know that she's not withholding something from you?" I'd hear one of two answers: "I just know" or "I've never thought about that. I guess I'll have to ask her."

I celebrate the closeness of women who trust that their mother would tell them all their secrets. I've also heard enough stories to know that it's still worth having a conversation about secrets, especially if you haven't had one in a while. If nothing comes of your talk, the outcome will give you a sense of freedom and confirm that there are no taboo tales to be told. If it turns out that there is something you need to know and your mother has been withholding information, at the very least you've created an opening for her to reveal herself.

How Do You Talk to Your Mother About Secrets?

You've determined that you want to talk to your mother about a secret you think she may be keeping from you, or you have a secret to tell her. Or you simply want to revisit an old secret that still troubles you. What do you do next?

Write this down. *Do not say to your mother, "Are you keeping any secrets from me?" or "I have a secret to tell you."* These two openings are guaranteed to cause you problems and shut down communication immediately. Disclosing difficult information takes preparation, timing, and open language.

Your preparation will include calming your fears around talking to your mother about either of your secrets, writing out a script, and finishing your rehearsal by visualizing a positive outcome. You don't want to leave an important conversation like this to chance. One of the major reasons communication breaks down and relationships fail is that people don't think through all the logical consequences and emotions that will arise from an important disclosure. The more options you walk yourself through, the better your chances are of finding out what you need to know or make known.

Write down in your journal what you're most afraid of in either hearing your mother's secret or telling her your secret. Are you worried that she has cancer? Financial problems? Are you ashamed of having to tell her you're getting a divorce? Are you angry that she hasn't told you about your brother's drug problem? Be honest with yourself. If you begin your conversation without acknowledging to yourself what your hidden feelings are, I can guarantee you that those feelings will show up and could sabotage all your efforts. Emotions always play a part in secret keeping; fear and anger are the major reasons most people don't want to tell secrets.

Once you've identified your feelings, the next step is to ask yourself what you think she'll say and determine an appropriate answer that will keep communication open.

Following are four common responses your mother might give you when you ask her about a secret you think she's keeping and a word-for-word reply that you can say in return to maintain an open dialogue.

Mother: I don't want to talk about it.

Daughter: Mom, I can see that this upsets you, and as much as you don't want to talk about it, I need to. I'd really appreciate your helping me through this so that we can resolve things and move on to subjects that are more pleasant for both of us.

Mother: That's none of your business.

Daughter: Mom, if I were you, I think I might feel exactly the same way and [not *but*] I'd still like to talk to you about this. It's important to me to know what happened. As much as you think the truth will hurt me, I'd rather know and be able to make my own choices than keep blaming you for withholding information from me.

Mother: I can't talk about that.

Daughter: I can appreciate your choice to say nothing. If and when you're ready to talk about it, I'll be here for you.

Or:

Mom, help me to understand why this is off-limits to you. If I understand, I'll be better able to let this go, and maybe in conversations down the road, you'll realize it's okay to share more with me.

Mother: Why would you want to know that?

This is a deflection technique. Your mother is either buying time or hoping to put an end to the conversation, most likely because she feels she's being interrogated or doesn't want to give you an answer. Keep your voice calm, start with one of the following phrases, and lead directly back to the question you were asking.

Daughter: I'm curious, Mom, and I want to understand you and myself better. Now, what was really going on when . . . ?

Or:

Because I really want to understand you better. Now . . .

Or:

Because I'm really interested. Now . . .

Get out your journal and open to two blank pages. On the left-hand page, write down what you think your mother will say when you ask her to disclose her secret. On the right-hand side, write down what you'll say in return. Use Terri's response below as a guide.

Terri: Mom, I've really been struggling with something that I hope you can help me understand better.

Mother: What?

Terri: [Describes actual behavior very specifically] Well, I've been really worried about you lately. I noticed that you haven't been calling me as much as you used to, and I noticed a stack of bills on the counter the last time I was here. It's not like you to let bills pile up. I also over-heard you mention to Aunt Jean on the phone that you didn't know how you were going to pay your medical bills. Whatever is going on, I'm hoping you'll clear things up for me.

Mother: It's all under control.

Terri: Mom, I hear you saying that you've got a handle on it, but I'm still worried. I'd like to help you, but I can't if you don't tell me what's going on.

Mother: Well, I didn't want to bother you.

Terri: Mom, you're not bothering me. Whatever is going on, we can solve this easier and faster together.

Mother: I thought I could handle it, but with the surgery I had last year and still being a year away from Medicare and retire-ment, I don't know how I'm going to cover all my bills. I'm feeling really anxious about this and haven't known how to talk to you children because I don't want to be a burden.

Terri: [Keeping it light] Mom, I am so relieved to hear that. I didn't know if you were gambling, playing the horses, or

	spending all your money on lottery tickets. I'm guessing that you're feeling really worried about all this and that it's making you feel like withdrawing from everyone. How about if we brainstorm some options for you? I have a friend who's a financial planner, and she's really good with helping seniors manage their money.
Mother:	That's would be a great relief. Thank you.

Terri managed to keep herself calm and reassure her mother. Instead of telling her mother what to do, she offered suggestions along with gentle guidance. She succeeded because she prepared and practiced.

Your actual conversation will be different from what you wrote, but thinking through your mother's objections ahead of time and your responses will give you an edge. Talk to successful sports coaches and they'll tell you that before the actual game they always walk their team through as many scenarios as possible so that they know what to do if the situation presents itself. This practice will also free your mind to make spontaneous and healthy choices when you're in conversation with your mother.

The last thing you want to make sure you do before you talk with your mom is visualize a positive outcome. Turn your worry inside out, and imagine the best that could happen. Think of your mother as a close friend. How would you interact with a friend who seemed as if she needed to talk but didn't know how to open the subject up for discussion? You'd gently say at the appropriate time, "It seems like you have something on your mind. If you want to talk about anything, I'm glad to listen to you."

What Secrets Are You Keeping from Your Mother?

When you peer into the deepest, darkest closets of your mind, is there anything that you never want your mother to know? Is there anything you wish you could tell your mother? You'll want to answer these questions because inevitably when you talk to your mother about her secrets, she's going to ask you about yours. You want to be prepared.

Candace was eight years old when a neighbor sexually molested her at the local park. She had been taught to respect her elders, so although she remembers that what he did hurt her and it wasn't right, she followed his orders, including not telling anyone.

In her forties, Candace developed chronic fatigue and was cared for by her mother, Marie, for several months. During this time, Candace and Marie spent a lot of time talking, and Candace told her mother about the incident with the neighbor. Marie, concerned and hurt, asked, "Why didn't you tell me?" Candace told her she kept the secret because the neighbor had told her not to tell anyone. Marie didn't ask any more questions, which was a relief to Candace, who said, "I didn't tell my mom this, but the real reason I was afraid to tell her back then was because I thought I would have been punished by her for not getting up and leaving. I decided that there was nothing to be gained by telling her now about my fear because she did the best she could, and I didn't need to burden her with guilt. I had worked it out in therapy and felt no anger toward her and certainly didn't need to cause her more pain about something from the past."

Candace took a big step in telling her mother what she thought was most important for her to know: that the incident happened and that her mother's intuitions were accurate about the neighbor. But Candace stopped short of giving her mother her deeper truth, and thereby she eliminated the opportunity for her mother to empathize with Candace's fear and shame or to take responsibility for her own feelings. Candace could have said something like this: "That was a really scary situation. I didn't know how to tell you that I was also afraid you'd punish me for letting him do that to me. It's hard for me to believe that I felt that way when I was little because I feel so close to you now. I finally learned in therapy that it's normal for children to feel they're responsible for what happened and to fear that their parents would punish them instead of protect them."

I recommend talking through your pain directly with your mother whenever possible—and if necessary—in a therapist's office. It may not be easy, but the possibility for healing is too great to dismiss.

Carol, a scientist, noticed her mother pulling away from her when she told her that she was a lesbian. Although they remained on speaking terms, all phone calls and visits with her mother remained at a superficial level, with no discussion of Carol's personal life. When Carol and her partner, Janet, decided to make a lifelong commitment to each other, Carol called her parents, who live in another state. Her father said adamantly, "I'm not coming, but if your mother wants to, that's her decision." Carol's mother, Nancy, also declined to attend, saying, "I can't do this. There's nothing more to talk about." Carol, although terribly hurt, remained composed and said to her mother, "I hear you, and I can accept that. But you are never not going to know what's going on in my life because I don't tell you. It's only if you choose not to know. I'm not going to hide my truth from you. You can only do that yourself."

Several months following Carol and Janet's commitment ceremony, Carol went home to visit her mother on her birthday. The two women took a walk in her mother's favorite woods. Nancy said to Carol, "I'm so glad you made time to be here. I wanted you to be able to hear the wind." Carol recalls, "What a gift my mother gave me on that day, in that moment. A gift of a place where we could fully meet and a reminder that even when we cannot fully meet because of boundaries we both need to have, we can still hear the wind. We can pause to listen to it and feel it and know we are loved with a strength that is even greater than the distance that separates us."

Risking a mother's rejection has to be one of the most threatening situations in which we can put ourselves. Carol's decision to continue to stay open and not withhold information from her mother was a courageous response to her mother's inability to accept her choices. While some of us may not choose to be that forgiving, Carol has created an opening for her mother to change her mind. Sometimes that is the best and only thing we can do to strengthen and heal our relationship with our mother.

In her book *Love, Ellen*, Betty DeGeneres tells the story of coming to terms with a secret her daughter, comedienne Ellen DeGeneres, told her when Ellen was twenty: "Mom, I'm gay." For the next twenty years, until Ellen publicly announced her sexual preference on her show, *Ellen*, Betty remained personally supportive and publicly mute. She writes:

Having to keep any kind of secret can become a terrible burden. But, on the other hand, given my years of early training with Mother's warnings—"Don't tell Aunt Ethel"—I really know how to keep secrets. It wasn't my place to share this information about my daughter. That had to be Ellen's choice.

So, along with everything else we had survived together, perhaps the secret brought us even closer. Whatever we did or did not share with the outer world, with each other we became very honest and open.

When Ellen decided to come out publicly in 1997, Diane Sawyer of *Primetime Live* interviewed Ellen's entire family. Betty writes, "I had no idea how pivotal my taking part in this interview was going to be in my own life's journey. I only knew how liberating it felt to be rid of a twenty-year-old secret."

Sharing your secret can be empowering, as it clearly was for Carol, Ellen, and Betty. All three women took responsibility for their beliefs. They were willing to endure the fear, rejection, and loss that a choice that goes against the prevailing culture entails, and in the end they triumphed. You can too when you take the risk to be true to yourself and allow your mother to do the same.

Revisiting Old Secrets

Secrets are funny things. There's a part of us that would rather die than expose our deepest, darkest self to another person, and yet there's also a part of us that desperately wants to be found out and loved in spite of our shadows. Helping another person find the safety and acceptance to bare her soul is one of the greatest gifts we give that person. It is also one of the most challenging when the secret revolves around something that involves us. I am constantly reminded of this dichotomy when I am flying to or from a speaking engagement. Squished into those seats like wrinkled clothes in a closet that's too full, I've heard more about the intimate lives of people I'll never see again than I've ever heard from my family and friends. These ephemeral acts of confession by my seatmates usually end with, "I've never told anyone this," or "I can tell you because you're not my mother [child, spouse, boss . . .]." If only we found it this easy to talk to our mothers.

We can, if we plan ahead and have the patience to see this as a life-long process instead of a one-time event. If you haven't had the type of closeness where you can pick up wherever you left off no matter how long it's been between visits, it will take time to develop. And realistically there are some situations where, sadly, this will not happen. But this is not reason to give up hope. The universe has a very interesting way of taking care of our needs when we're at an impasse or crossroads, as Debbie found.

My friend Debbie is a gifted high school counselor and married mother of two young boys. Her mother, Mary, was an alcoholic who told Debbie her birth father died in a plane crash in the Korean War. An only child raised by her grandmother because her mother was too ill to care for her, Debbie grew up always wondering about her father. When she was eighteen, Debbie's grandmother died. On her deathbed, her grandmother told Debbie that her father hadn't died in the Korean War and was not the man stated on her birth certificate. Debbie asked for his name, but her grandmother told her that the rest of the story would have to come from Debbie's mother, because her mother had refused to divulge Debbie's father's name to anyone.

Knowing her mother's behavior was irrational and hurtful, Debbie sought out as much information as she could before confronting her mother, who lived apart from Debbie and her grandmother. Armed with her birth certificate, she arranged a visit with her mother. During the visit she said, "Mom, I need to know the truth about my father. What is his name?" Her mother refused to answer the question, saying it was none of Debbie's business. Over the next eighteen years, Mary refused to give her daughter the information she so desperately wanted. Debbie came to understand many things about her mother that were very painful, including that her mother felt so little control in her own life that having a secret that Debbie didn't know allowed her mother to feel more powerful.

After years of stressful encounters trying to find the truth Debbie finally said, "I have to let this go. I may never know who my real father is, and that's just the way it is." When I asked Debbie how she found the strength to get through this horror, she said, "I have a wonderful husband and children. At least I know what not to do with them."

Debbie's story points out that there is always a chance that you may not find out what you need to know, no matter how hard you try or how "right" you do things. That's a hard lesson to learn, but if we embrace the lesson and our life and find other people to help us through the storm, we can meet the challenge. If your efforts fail and you don't get what you need, do not give up hope in other people; answers show up in the strangest ways when you least expect them, as Debbie found out shortly before her mother died.

Called away on a business trip for a week, Debbie, now in her mid-thirties, was anxious about going away because of her mother's condition. Debbie's husband, Gus, reassured her that he would handle any emergencies and call her immediately if there were any changes in her mother's health. While Debbie was gone, Mary took a turn for the better and was released from the hospital. Gus went to pick her up and as a goodwill gesture took her to dinner before dropping her off at her apartment. During dinner, she divulged to Gus who Debbie's real father was. Mary died two weeks later. Within the year, Debbie was able to locate her father and make a connection. A few years later, she discovered a half-sister and is now working on opening the door to other siblings.

Had Debbie chosen to keep the secret from her husband, who knows if she would have ever been able to break the code and discover the truth. As she continues her life, she moves carefully and slowly to change a pattern of secrets that has been in her family for generations. It is a lifelong journey that requires patience, trust, and the willingness to endure setbacks and heartbreaks along the way. But the potential rewards are tremendous: self-acceptance, freedom, and joy. Be brave in your search. Your legacy is in your hands.

*You gain strength, courage, and confidence by every experience
in which you really stop to look fear in the face. You are able to
say to yourself, "I lived through this horror. I can take the next
thing that comes along. . . ." You must do the thing you think
you cannot do.*

—ELEANOR ROOSEVELT,
You Learn by Living

Activities to Do with Your Mom

❑ Plan a time when the two of you can be alone, uninterrupted, for at
least an hour.
  - Take a walk in the park.
  - Ask to talk in her bedroom, and lie on the bed like teenagers.
  - Sit in your car and talk outside the house. Studies show that sit-
    ting side by side rather than directly across from each other
    eases conflict.
  - Bake together.
❑ Write a letter about your concerns, and read it to her.
❑ Go through old photo albums together, and ask her to tell you her
memories. When she gets to the places where you want more detail,
say, "Tell me more about that. I'm still fuzzy about that time."
❑ Go back to your childhood neighborhood, and walk around to-
gether.

Questions to Ask Your Mom

- What's one of the best or most fun secrets you've been a part of?
- Have you ever told another person's secret to someone else and then
  had the original secret teller find out you'd betrayed that confidence? What did you do?
- Did you ever divulge anyone else's secret to protect that person
  from harm?
- Under what circumstances would you want me to tell you a secret?

- Under what circumstances would you not want me to tell you a secret?
- What really happened when . . . ?
- How did you really feel when I left home and went to college [started working, got married, got a divorce]?
- What have you always wanted to ask me but were afraid to?
- I've always wanted to ask you about . . .
- Are there any secrets I need to know for health reasons? Is there alcoholism or depression in our family that I don't know about?
- Can I check this out with you? I remember hearing this secret a long time ago that's been whispered around the family, and I just wanted to know what your perspective is on it.
- Have you ever been really glad that you told a secret? What were the circumstances?

Show Me the Way to Go Home

Aging

Growing older isn't what it used to be. Advances in technology and medicine have come a long way in helping women live longer, healthier lives. The average woman's life span in 1919 was fifty-four; today it is eighty-four, and climbing every decade. Women of age are stepping into the spotlight, and society is better for it. Just last week, here in San Diego, Barbara Bush and Margaret Thatcher were part of a panel of great leaders along with several well-respected businessmen. But along with the spotlight comes a shadow: our American culture's obsession with youth and beauty and the consequential shunning of the elderly, in particular, older women. Betty Friedan, a leader in the women's movement, in her book *The Fountain of Age*, identifies this shadow as the "Age Mystique"—the myth that aging is about physical and mental decline. Aging, according to Friedan, is more than our health problems; aging is an adventure filled with opportunities for a deepening sense of intimacy and purpose in life. We can live vitally to our death if we're willing to reframe the reality of aging from one of searching for the eternal fountain of youth to seeking out the fountain of age.

Friedan's belief about viewing aging as an adventure was born out of turning sixty herself. Her family gave her a surprise birthday party, which made her feel that she was being pushed out of life "professionally, politically, personally, and sexually." She was depressed for weeks until she remembered the feisty, vibrant women she'd met following the publication of her book *The Feminine Mystique*. These women were older—at least fifty (this sounds so young to me!)—and had broadened their roles to include employee, entrepreneur, student, political activist, artist, as well as the traditional roles of wife and mother.

Today it seems quite normal for women to express a variety of roles, but it was a radical departure for women who entered the workforce when their husbands went off to World War II. Traditionally, women beyond childbearing years have been viewed as babysitters of grand-children and caregivers of aging spouses who retired. Retirement has an entirely different meaning for women today. Our mothers have many more options available to them in these years: political activism, community involvement, going back to school, turning a hobby into a business, or any other creative endeavor that appeals to her is available. If her health is good, as my mother used to say, "the sky's the limit."

Health and Longevity

Your mother's health is the most significant indicator of how well she will fare in her later years. According to the American Association of Retired Persons (AARP), which boasts over 30 million members:

- 33 percent of all people over the age of sixty-five report that they have fair to poor health and at least one chronic health problem that limits their daily activities.
- 50 percent of the population over the age of eighty-five, predominantly women, require help with basic living activities of eating, bathing, and dressing.
- 80 percent of caregivers for the elderly are the daughters of those elderly who are in their forties, with children of their own.
- Elder care will replace child care as the number one dependent-care issue in the workplace in the next ten years.

The good news here is that two-thirds of the older population (sixty-five and over) are healthy and mobile, and half of the elderly (eighty-five and over) are able to care for themselves. Hopefully your mother will be part of this thriving, active population, and her aging will be a positive experience for both of you. Regardless, it is important that you have a conversation with her about what her wishes are as she reaches her later years.

If your mother is actively enjoying her later years, this conversation will serve as a way to celebrate your mother's vitality with her and to draw out her wisdom. If your mother is struggling with the aging process or is in poor health, this topic will help you give her information and encouragement that will help renew her spirit.

> *Age is something that doesn't matter—unless you are a cheese.*
> —BILLIE BURKE, actress, in *Quotable Women of the Twentieth Century*

Many aspects of aging have come up in previous chapters, and some of the more spiritual aspects will come up later. But some other specific aspects of aging require their own discussion:

- What are your attitudes and beliefs about aging, and do they serve you and your mother?
- How does your mother feel about getting older, and how has that affected your own attitudes about aging?
- How does your mother want to live in her old age? Will she have mobility and housing issues to contend with? If so, what are your responsibilities, and how do you talk with her about them?
- What wisdom has your mother gained in aging, and what insights can she share with you to help you in your aging discovery and process?

> *There is nothing inherently wrong with a brain in your nineties. If you keep it fed and interested you'll find it lasts you very well.*
> —MARY STONEMAN DOUGLAS, *Mary Stoneman Douglas: Voices of the River*

Self-Fulfilling Prophecies

In the twenty years I have done research on how to live a more mean-ingful life, a sense of purpose appears in the top three characteristics in all studies. Purpose—the goals we strive toward, our raison d'être—is expressed in everything we think, say, and do. Some longevity experts even go so far as to say that how long we live and the quality of our lives is directly affected by our sense of purpose about life. An article in *Advances in Nursing Science* reports that one of the leading indicators of an older woman's satisfaction with her life is a sense of purpose and the possibilities a social network provides to express that purpose. Discovering what motivates your mother to get up in the morning and ac-knowledging her strengths will help reinforce her sense of significance and make both of your lives more enjoyable.

My mother's father wanted to live to be a hundred. That's purpose. He came very close, outliving my grandmother by almost two decades and thriving until he was ninety-eight. When he was in his late eighties, I was in my late teens. On Wednesday afternoons in the summer, I often drove him to the Shorewood Senior Center (he called it "Senior Recess") to play cards ("and meet chicks," he once told me). After one trip, I mused out loud to my mother, "Grandpa's really active for being such an old man. I wonder how long he'll live? Mom, how long do you want to live?" I wasn't prepared for her answer. She responded with more certainty than about most other subjects we discussed: "I don't want to live any longer than my mother. I don't want to go to a senior center and sit on a couch all day watching TV or playing cards with lots of old people. I want to be with young people. You're so much more fun." At the time, I brushed off her comment with a teen's sense of immortality.

Ten years later, my grandfather died. After his funeral, I asked Mom the question again. Her answer was the same: "Not any longer than my mother." I said nothing; I didn't know how to respond. Frankly I was scared. I was just learning about the power of purpose and self-fulfilling prophecies. If we're more powerful than we think, I won-dered, what does that say about how we live? For days after, I was silently preoccupied about my mother's death and what my beliefs were about my own life span. After Mom died, her comments floated into my awareness again. I looked up my grandmother's birth and death dates. Grandma died of cancer two days before her seventieth birthday. Mom died from cancer three months shy of turning seventy.

I wouldn't begin to predict all the variables involved in my mother's death, but I do know that when she learned of her cancer diagnosis two weeks before Thanksgiving, her fighting spirit came alive. She told us she had a mission: to celebrate Christmas and to live to see her third grandchild, who was expected around Easter. Jimmy was born seventy-two hours after Mom died.

How Do You Feel About Getting Older?

Take a few minutes to see what your beliefs are about aging with regard to your mother and yourself. Respond to the following statements in your journal, and simply notice what comes up. By checking in with yourself, you'll be better prepared to talk with your mother.

- What I most fear about getting older is . . .
- What I think my mother most fears about getting older is . . .
- What I'm most excited about with getting older is . . .
- What I think excites my mother most about being older is . . .
- What I have learned from my mother about aging is . . .
- When my mother is no longer able to care for herself, I will . . .
- When I am an old woman I will . . .

> *Old age is always fifteen years older than I am.*
> —Anonymous

Eighty-Three Is a Wonderful Age to Be Alive

Following the death of her husband, and with the encouragement of her two daughters, Edith Leech returned to school at the age of seventy-seven. She packed up her bags in Maryland, moved into a dormitory in Oakland, California, and attended Matthew Fox's University of Creation Spirituality. Intending to stay only a semester, Edith remained an entire year and was applauded as the oldest and one of the most involved students on campus. She now leads two weekly women's spirituality groups and remarks, "Aside from a few aches and pains, I'm blessed with a rich, full life. Eighty-three is a wonderful age to be alive."

Edith's positive attitude attracts people of all ages into her life. Her daughter Mary said that at a family wedding, she found her mother surrounded by several grandchildren and their friends, all of them in their twenties. She overheard one of the young men walk away saying, "She is really cool. I want to date her." Older women like Edith are needed for their wisdom, creativity, and experience to help shift outdated notions of older people.

Your mother may not know how much she is needed. Remind her of all the places where she can make a contribution: at-risk-children's centers, museums, hospitals, homeless shelters, hospices. Encourage her to start a new hobby: painting, writing her memoirs, gardening, or quilting. If she has lost her zest for living or is homebound, get her a computer and teach her how to use it. I run across many older women who say they're too old or too busy to use the computer, but when a computer appeared wrapped as a birthday or Mother's Day gift, and their daughters taught them how to use it, they were hooked. If she isn't sure what to do with the computer, remind her that there is work to be done lobbying Congress for better legislation regarding aging. Changes in insurance and medical benefits can't happen without people who use those systems expressing their concerns. There are on-line communities where she can network with others of all ages and interests. Much of this work can be done on-line in the comfort of your mother's own home. Your mother doesn't have to get involved if she's not interested, but she does deserve to know that the option for vital aging exists and she can be part of it if she chooses. Until this perspective is the norm for all women, aging will still be seen as a problem to be overcome rather than an adventure to embrace. We, as our mother's daughters, are the first line of defense in ensuring not just our mother's future, but also the future of all other women. When we take the time to talk with our mothers about getting older, we show them that their ideas and interests still matter, that they are not invisible, unnecessary, or a burden. We help remind them that turning seventy or eighty or ninety, even with health problems, can be a positive experience.

Just a Minute; I'm Having a Senior Moment

My mother has three surviving sisters, all in their late seventies and early eighties. All are vibrant women with the same wonderful sense of humor and energy as my mother. My Aunt Dorothy sold her home and moved into a condominium when her husband died. When I asked her what her lifestyle was like now that she was alone, she described an active life of family, friends, and travel. In the previous six months, even with knee replacement surgery (she's an avid tennis player), she had taken a three-week driving trip with her college roommate visiting friends on the East Coast, flown to Arizona for a ten-day visit with two of her brothers (ages eighty-four and sixty-four), been part of several family gatherings with her six children, met with her two bridge clubs once a month, swam at the Y once a week, and played golf at least once a week during the summer. When I asked her what she and her friends talked about when they played bridge, she said, "We've been getting together since all of us were first married. It's going on fifty years for some of us. Some of the women's husbands have died, but we still keep meeting. We talk about travel, our children, the latest health tips." And then she laughed and said, "And how many senior moments we're having."

"Senior moments? What are those?" I asked, expecting some comment about discussing treasured memories.

She laughed again and said, "When you can't remember what you just did or said. Oh, that reminds me, I've got another one. Yesterday I was at the Y and heard a new one in the pool: 'I'm experiencing an intellectual pause.'"

My aunt Dorothy is clearly enjoying her later years and mentions that the women she knows are active senior citizens who don't feel their age and don't pay attention to media fear campaigns about aging.

They make the most of what life presents them and enjoy their families and each other's company.

Community—whether it's immediate family or an extended network of friends in the neighborhood, at school, or at church—is a very important part of healthy aging. Dr. Andrew Weil, author of *Women's Health*, reported on Fox TV recently that the two most important factors in health and longevity are physical movement and a strong network of family and friends. If your mother is living in an isolated environment, arrange to get her out of the house. Even if she's in a wheelchair, get her out for walks. To a homebound person, a little fresh air, conversation, and a good hug make all the difference in the world.

When Your Mother's Husband Requires Care

If your mother is dealing with her husband's poor health and is his main caregiver, your involvement and support are critical, especially reminding her to take care of herself.

Karen's mother, Jean, in her early seventies, was in denial for several years about her husband's advancing Alzheimer's disease. Karen noticed her father's decline during her parents' yearly visit. Wanting to address the issue and make sure her mother acknowledged the worsening situation, Karen used empathy as a way to open the door. She recalls, "I took Mom out to a Thai restaurant for dinner without my dad. When she started talking about Dad's behavior at the beginning of the meal, I said, 'It must just be the worst.' She didn't say anything. I sensed she was keeping up a positive front and not wanting to burden me, which was exactly what I wanted to break through. I wanted to be a support to her. I made the comment twice more, weaving it into the conversation when she mentioned some of the things Dad did that annoyed her. When I said, 'It must just be the worst,' the third time, she lost it. She began to weep and said, 'You have no idea how hard it is.' That's when things began to change. She'd been dealing quietly with this for years, all the while continuing to run the company she and my father started. We talk about my Dad's situation all the time now. She's hired a nurse's aide to care for him and is working part time to keep her sanity. She feels terribly guilty but knows it's the right thing. She doesn't have the strength or mobility to care for him, but she still loves him deeply. She's learned to accept him where he is now and, I think, appreciates the person he's become, as well as who he was."

Break Through Your Mother's Resistance to Aging

Accepting the changes in others and ourselves that come with aging is one of the biggest challenges people face in growing older. Myths abound about aging gracefully, but everyone I've ever talked to says getting older is messy. Routines become important, but they're often disrupted, causing stress. You say good-bye to people, activities, and things you used to be able to do with ease. It's not always easy, and when it isn't, your mother may throw a few curve balls your way.

If you find your mother a little more distant, irritable, or needy, your tendency may be to start telling her what to do or talking to her like a child. Be careful; you do so at the risk of shutting down communication. Mark Edinberg, author of *Talking with Your Aging Parents*, writes, "Treating adults like children implies they are likely to disobey and be uncooperative." If you want results with your mother, remember that even in her neediness or resistance, she is still an adult who wants to be treated with respect.

Following are five phrases that adult children often hear their parents saying when they reach the age where mobility and independence are issues. Following each statement is a description of what's really going on, what your mother needs from you in that moment, and what you can say to diffuse the tension and ease her frustration.

When Your Mother Says, "I Don't Want to Burden You"

What's going on: Her maternal instinct is kicking in to protect you.

What your mother needs:

- To know that she is important to you and not an inconvenience.
- To know you'll be there if she needs you.
- To hear you tell her that you will do what she needs.

What to say in response:

❑ "Mom, I know you may feel like a burden, but you are my mother and I will always do whatever I can to help you."
❑ "Mom, what do you need right now? If I can't help you, I'm sure we can find someone else who can."

When Your Mother Says, "It's Not So Bad"

What's going on: Your mother may be in denial and downplaying a bad situation.

What your mother needs:

- For you to pay closer attention to her. Check for depression (see Conversation 1).
- For you to step in and assess how serious the situation really is.

What to say in response:

❑ "Mom, are you sure this is okay for you? I wouldn't be able to tolerate it."
❑ "Mom, it sounds as if you're sugarcoating this situation. Is it really not so bad?"

When Your Mother Says, "Stop Treating Me Like a Child"

What's going on: Your mother is resisting letting go of control, or you have overstepped your boundaries with her.

What your mother needs:

- To maintain as much independence as possible.
- To see you step back and stop parenting her so much.

What to say in response:

❑ "Mom, it sounds as if you're frustrated by the way I'm treating you. Is that what's going on, or is there something else on your mind?"
❑ "Mom, I may be overstepping my bounds here, but from what I can see, this is what we need to do. What do you think is the best way to handle this?"

When Your Mother Says, "I Can Do This Myself."

What's going on: She needs to feel that she is still capable of caring for herself.

What your mother needs:

- For you to do a self-check: Are you trying to do too much for her? Are you in a hurry and trying to rush her? Do you need to be more patient?
- For you to give her a chance to do it herself before you rush in to save her.

What to say in response:

❑ "Of course, you can. I may be overreacting because I want you to be safe."
❑ "I'm happy to do this for you. Why don't you let me help you?"
❑ "I'm sorry to have to push this, Mom. I know you want to do this for yourself, but I don't have time right now to wait for you to do this, so please work with me here and let me help you."

**When Your Mother Says, "What Do You Mean,
I Can't Drive Anymore?"**

What's going on: Your mother wants to control her life and mobility.

What your mother needs:

- To be safe, to maintain her independence.
- For you to be very specific in what you're noticing about her driving and point out the safety factors involved, helping her come to her own decision to stop driving.
- For you to keep her safe and take away her keys if necessary.

What to say in response:

- ❑ "Mom, I know how much you value your independence, but I want you to think for a moment about how you almost caused an accident today. It's not safe for you to continue driving. Please, let's figure out other options for you."
- ❑ "Mom, I know this is really hard for you, but this is not an option. You can no longer drive. Your eyesight and response time are no longer good enough to keep you and other people on the road safe."

I Don't Want to Go to a Nursing Home

Mobility and housing issues will eventually be an issue for your mother unless she maintains her health, owns her own home, and has the income to hire a home health nurse to care for her until she dies. Hopefully your mother will be active and mentally fit until her death, but this is not the norm when women enter their elderly years (eighty-five and older). Having a conversation with your mother when she enters the beginning of old age (sixty-five to seventy-four) about her wishes when she becomes too infirm to care for herself will be of great help to both of you.

My mother—like many other mothers I've come across in my research—often said, "I don't want to be a burden to my children." I always felt that included in that statement was a subliminal message that said, "But you better take care of me after all I've done for you." As I began to talk with her more honestly, I realized how frightening it was for her to lose her mobility and struggle day by day to let go of another piece of herself. I also learned that the more satisfied you feel about the life you've lived and the more risks you've taken, the less fear you feel as you encounter the changing faces of age.

During one of my mother's anxious moments following an emergency visit to the hospital several years before she died, she pleaded with me, "I don't want to go to a nursing home. Ever! Promise you won't put me in a nursing home?" I felt tremendous internal conflict because I couldn't imagine caring for her full time and didn't want to upset her more than she already was. I paused a moment too long before I said, "Of course, we won't." I could tell from the look in her eyes and her silence that she wasn't convinced. Neither was I.

In the weeks following that conversation with my mother, I walked myself through several future scenarios of caring for her: in my home, at her home, and in a nursing home. None of them was pleasant or comforting.

When my mother needed spinal surgery a few years later, I called my siblings together to discuss what we would do if Mom needed long-term nursing care following her surgery. We decided that if my father was not able to care for her, we would put her in a nursing home. It was a sobering conversation. I prayed that we wouldn't have to make that decision, knowing that Mom would feel betrayed by all of us.

I Could Never Put Mom in a Home. I'll Take Care of Her

Memories of my conversation with my mother and my siblings resurfaced when we gathered again to discuss Mom's long-term care after she was diagnosed with cancer. I remember my sister Eileen speaking first: "I could never put Mom in a home. I'll take care of her." I wanted to stand up and applaud her courage. Originally, like the rest of us, she had been willing to provide financial support but didn't want to be my mother's caregiver. My sister's willingness, commitment, and courage inspired the rest of us to make the right choice for Mom and our family. With Eileen at the helm, we were able to care at home for my mother, and later my father, until their deaths.

As I listen to friends face similar decisions, I'm glad I don't have to make that decision again—until it's my own turn. If you need to talk to your mother about long-term care, choose a relaxed time to bring up the subject. Consider saying the following to open your conversation: "Mom, I'd like to talk with you about your living arrangements in the future should something happen to you or me. It's important to me that you're well provided for, so I'd like to know what the perfect arrangement would look like for you. Would you like to talk about it now, or take a few days to think about it?"

I Don't Know If I Want a Croning. What Is It?

On her sixtieth birthday author Betty Friedan took herself on at Outward Bound wilderness expedition for people over age fifty-five. Her goal was clear: to break out of her dread and denial of age and celebrate her milestone birthday. She lived to tell the story and learned that it was possible to go beyond the perceived limits of age. She writes in *The Fountain of Age*, "I had a hunger now for further adventures 'beyond'— spiritual and intellectual, as well as physical."

Adventures of the body, mind, and spirit are growing in popularity almost as quickly as physical exploration. In particular, one spiritual adventure is that of croning, an ancient ritual used to acknowledge a woman's wisdom when she became an elder in the community. "In ancient times," says Edna Ward, editor of *Celebrating Ourselves, A Crone Ritual Book*, "old women were known as crones. They held power and enjoyed status as the healers, the mediators, and the wise of the communities. Gradually, that power and recognition were lost. In modern times, the old woman has become nearly invisible, pushed aside and forgotten. The rising interest in croning ceremonies also reflects a larger movement to reassert the value of older women."

For their mother's eightieth birthday, Mary and Lynn thought it would be special to give Edith a croning. When Mary posed the question to her mother, she responded, "I don't know if I want a croning.

What is it?" After Mary explained the ceremony, Edith replied, "Maybe. Let me think about it." A few days later, she said yes. (As we age, our need for more decision-making time increases. Keep this in mind, and give your mother more time to make decisions).

The night of the ritual, eighteen friends—including women in their forties, fifties, and sixties—arrived at Edith's home to celebrate her croning. Mary emceed the evening, played special music, and presented Edith with a purple shawl (the color purple represents wisdom) and a reading on what it means to be a crone. Edith then performed her own ritual, speaking of the parts of herself that she wanted to let go of, including fear and resistance to change. Following the letting-go process, she spoke about what she was claiming for herself, such as courage and insight. After Edith finished, each of her friends took a turn lighting a candle and sharing how Edith was a "wise woman" for them. All the women commented that the ritual created an opening for them to embrace their own wise woman. Edith was ecstatic and said it was one of the most meaningful events of her life.

Two days later, Mary and Lynn orchestrated a traditional birthday party with eighty friends and family. The entire weekend was a way to reframe the message that unless you're in the creative motherly stage, you're useless. Celebrating the crone in all women acknowledges that women of age are a fountain of endless creativity.

> *That advice to "act your age" is about the worst advice I ever heard. I'm always thinking, "What am I going to do when I grow up?" It's as if I haven't done anything yet. I would say to all women, "Don't give up your dreams and your desires. Don't give up the ship. Don't give up. Just keep on."*
> —LIZ SMITH, *On Women Turning Seventy*

Activities to Do with Your Mom

❑ Take a course together at the local university.
❑ Do an Outward Bound program.

❑ Watch movies together on women growing older as a segue into talking about personal beliefs, concerns, and benefits of growing older:

- *Driving Miss Daisy*, a touching story about the relationship between a wealthy elderly woman and her chauffeur in the American South
- *On Golden Pond*, the trials and tribulations of an adult daughter as she interacts with her elderly parents during a summer vacation
- *The Trip to Bountiful*, a moving story about an older woman whose adult children don't want her to travel and how she escapes to visit her childhood home
- *Fried Green Tomatoes*, about an elderly woman in a nursing home who helps a middle-aged woman become more assertive in her marriage as she tells a story of a friendship between two women in the 1920s

❑ Write a poem or letter listing all the things you've learned from your mother. Ask your mother to write a list of the wisdom she wants to leave you.

❑ Perform a croning ritual.

❑ Visit an assisted living community and a nursing home.

Questions for Your Mom

- How did your mother age? Physically? Emotionally? Mentally?
- How did you feel about your mother getting older?
- Whom do you admire who is older than you are? Why?
- What kind of old woman do you want to be?
- What's the best bit of wisdom you've recently heard from someone older than you?
- What regrets do you have, if any?
- What are the positive aspects of aging to you?
- If you were to go back to school, what would you study?
- What activities, trips, or courses would you like to do that you're not doing now?

- If you could go back and relive one moment, one month, or one year of your life, which would it be, and why?
- If you could change one thing about getting older, what would it be?
- What is your perfect living arrangement as you grow older? To live independently? In an assisted living community? With me?
- How would you like to celebrate your birthday this year? At sixty-five? Seventy? Seventy-five? Eighty? Eighty-five? Ninety? Would you like a croning celebration?
- What is one phrase that best sums up your experience of life at this age?
- When people think of you, what three things would you want them to remember?

Amazing Grace

Spirituality

Spiritual and religious rituals and traditions have long been a way that every culture has made sense of its world. The mysteries and miracles of life provide ample opportunity to attach meaning to our lives. We encounter moments that leave us awestruck, grateful, and occasionally frightened. How we interpret these events becomes the spiritual backbone that shapes who we become and how we live out our lives.

When things are going smoothly, our faith—in whatever we believe to be true—is invisible, carrying us in the current of creation. We speed along, not sure when we'll hit the rapids or traverse a waterfall, but we trust that we are moving in the right direction. It may not be safe; in fact, it may be quite dangerous. But our faith acts as a life jacket, keeping us from drowning in the unknown, the mundane, and the difficult.

Knowing what we believe in spiritually and having ways to express those beliefs create confidence in uncertain and chaotic times. From a simple prayer of thanks hastily whispered while running for a bus, to complex rituals and rules, we choose our spiritual paths in individual ways.

Spiritual meaning is different for everyone. Some people relate through intellect, some through nature, some pray, some perform rituals. Some meditate, others run marathons.
—JOAN BORYSENKO, PH.D.,
A Woman's Journey to God

When I speak of spirituality and spiritual beliefs in this chapter, I mean the entire range of experiences beyond the tangible and explainable. These include but are not limited to religion and religious beliefs. Miracles, the power of love, visions, as well as intuitive, telepathic, and psychic experiences, and our connection to animals and nature are also ways of connecting to spirit.

We all receive spiritual beliefs from our parents. Some of us stick with them throughout our entire life. Others of us are raised with one set of spiritual principles, only to embrace new ones upon reaching adulthood. Some of us try on churches and their spiritual leaders the way we try on clothes, discarding them when we've outgrown or grown tired of them. Our spiritual life is one place that is truly our own—until we share it with others.

Like politics, money, sex, and private matters, talking about our spiritual beliefs with anyone has tremendous emotional power, and particularly so with our mother. We want her to approve of our choices. We want her to understand and agree with us. For some women, that is easy. Sharing prayers, reading scripture, and singing favorite hymns together are part of the sweetness of life. For others, discussing religion with their mother is like paying double for a ticket to board the *Titanic*.

So why talk with your mother if you already share the same beliefs or it's going to be disastrous? If you share similar spiritual views, you'll reinforce and enrich what you already share together by asking the questions at the end of this chapter. If you've never talked with your mother about spirituality, you will take your relationship to a deeper and more meaningful level, and you'll learn things about her that you didn't know. If the two of you differ in your beliefs and the differences cause friction, the suggestions and questions in this chapter will help you both better understand each other's choices, which will clear the air in a healing way. In all cases, I recommend discussing spiritual beliefs and issues because someday you may need to make some difficult choices, and you'll be clear about what to do. Spiritual beliefs are at the root of every person's choices. Your mother's choices influence not just her life but also your own.

If you want to make God laugh, tell her your plans.
—Anonymous

Everyone Comes to God in Her Own Way

My own spiritual beliefs are eclectic, encompassing elements and rituals from many different religions. If I were pressed to declare an organized religion, I'd have to make up my own. Mostly I am a seeker. I want
to know that God exists. I continually search for evidence, marveling at
those who, like my mother, have never questioned their faith. I have
experienced what I call miracles—moments of love, grace, beauty,
wonder, and awe in the midst of the unexplainable—which I choose to
see as God's presence in my life.

I am the product of a strict Catholic upbringing, as were my parents.
I have an uncle who is a Jesuit priest, an uncle who is a Christian
brother, and an aunt who is a Notre Dame nun. From first through
eighth grade, I attended mass every morning—sometimes twice if I
went to 6:30 mass with my mother before school started. If it weren't
for the "no-talking-out-loud-for-the-rest-of-your-life" rule, I'd have become a novice (a nun before she takes her vows) in the Little Sister of
St. Theresa of the Flower Cloistered Carmelite Order when I was in
the seventh grade.

> *It would be easier to peel off a three-day-old Band-Aid from a
> hairy kneecap than to remove the patina of Baptist upbringing
> that coats my psyche.*
> —MARY ELLEN SNODGRASS,
> in *Ms.* magazine

When I entered high school, the daily mass stopped, but religion
classes continued. Unbeknown to my parents until I became engaged
(premarital counseling), I dropped out of the Catholic religion one
Sunday morning in April during my senior year in high school. It was
my birthday weekend, 1971. I took my mother to her first hootenanny
mass with guitar players and folk singers at my high school. As
the priest gave the sermon, he read a list of servicemen in the area who

had been killed in the Vietnam War that month. I experienced my first existential crisis.

While teenagers and parents around me were singing "Kumbayah," my mind was drowning with the heretical thought that there was no God. How could God allow these innocent young men and Vietnamese people to die for an unjust cause? I felt betrayed by this invisible father who had promised to bring salvation into the world through his children—children who continued to kill each other. I was scared by my thoughts but didn't feel safe enough to talk to anyone about them, lest I find myself in the afterlife with permanent residency in a very hot place for heresy. Unable to find an answer in the priest's sermon, I left church, had a birthday brunch at the Milky Way hamburger drive-in with my mother, and began my search for God.

> *I have come to know that God can dream a bigger dream for you than you can dream for yourself. And that the whole role for your life on Earth is to attach yourself to that force which is divine and let yourself be released to that.*
>
> —OPRAH WINFREY, in *Vogue*

My spiritual quest grew to include a broad range of explorations, which included attending the services of most major religions. I still attend mass when I am with my extended family for holidays and special occasions, such as baptisms, weddings, and funerals. I have been both affirmed and spooked by readings done by astrologers, channelers, and psychics. I spent five years in the mid-1980s researching the metaphysical aspects of color and music on people's health, as well as translating people's birth names into computerized musical compositions that could be used for meditation and focus.

My father often worried that my interests were cult oriented and would brainwash me into devil worship. My mother, much to my pleasure—while always affirming her faith in God and the Catholic religion and telling me she wished I would too—was curious about my journey and enjoyed hearing about what she called my "escapades." She said everyone comes to God in her own way, and that although she worried, she prayed for me and trusted that I'd find my way. It didn't occur to me until after her death that her name alone, Grace Rose, should have been a big enough clue that she was a walking, talking angel of hope.

She'd be pleased to know that I am talking with God these days. More and more often I have these frozen moments—while walking at the ocean, writing, petting my cat or a dog, hearing my nephews or my audience laugh, or being touched by someone's kindness—when I feel a quiet, peaceful presence melt over me, or a bubbling up of joy that suddenly bursts in my heart. In an instant I am replenished. Energy surges through my body. I breathe in, look up, throw my arms up into the sky, and shout in ecstasy, "Thank you, God!"

What Are Your Spiritual Beliefs?

Before you talk with your mother, it's important to know what your own spiritual beliefs are. What does spirituality mean to you? How do you envision God? What do you think happens after death? Your clarity will guide you in your discussion, as well as provide your mother with a framework in which to express herself. It may even inspire her to go deeper with her own understanding of her beliefs.

Answer these sentence completions in your journal:

• The best way to describe my spiritual beliefs is . . .
• The best way I can describe God is . . .
• I feel most connected to a higher power when . . .
• What I think happens after death is . . .
• When I am unable to make sense of tragedy or loss, I turn to . . .
• One of the most mystical or spiritual experiences I've had is . . .

Now that you've written your thoughts down, read them out loud to yourself. You want to be really comfortable with your answers and able to articulate yourself clearly. The more at ease you are in expressing yourself, the more opportunity there is for spontaneous, open, and ongoing dialogue with your mother.

> *I believe that God is in me as the sun is in the color and*
> *fragrance of a flower—the Light in my darkness, the Voice in*
> *my silence.*
> —HELEN KELLER, *Midstream*

I'm Going to Keep Praying for Your Souls

Alice, a women's health advocate and a single mother of a seventeen-year-old daughter, has opinions about religion that are very different from her mother's. Raised a Catholic, she watched her mother suffer through an abusive marriage because of her mother's commitment to her marriage vows. Alice still believes in a higher power but moved away from formalized religion when she was twenty-one, following the birth of her daughter and subsequent divorce.

Through the years, Alice and her mother, Rita, have had heated conversations about the differences in their religious beliefs that have ended with Rita giving Alice the silent treatment, followed by a letter stating how upset she is with her daughter.

Following one discussion that left both women cool toward each other for weeks, Alice realized she had two options in dealing with her mother: continue with the polarizing behavior or choose to reframe her mother's intention. "In my need to stay true to myself, I lost sight of my mother's need to protect me and my daughter," Alice recalled. "As soon as I remembered that she loved me and wanted the best for me, it was easier to express myself and not get hooked into her excessive worry that my daughter and I would go to hell.

"The next time I visited my mother, the first thing she said to me was, 'Alice, I need to speak with you. You've been blessed with a child.' I knew what was coming next, so instead of arguing with her, I said, 'Mom, you're right. I have been blessed with a beautiful daughter. I've also been blessed with other things too—good health, a roof over my head, a really good job, and the ability to take care of her.'

"Mom went on saying, '*You baptized your daughter* and agreed to raise her in the Catholic faith.'

"I acknowledged what she said again, 'Yes, I did agree with that. But *I was twenty years old then, and now I'm thirty-seven.* I see things differently now that I've learned more about what's important to me. I'm choosing not to raise my daughter with a religion that chooses to worship an unforgiving God, a religion that demoralizes women and tells them that they are less than men.'

"Mom wasn't happy with what I said. When she's upset with me, she'll keep talking, but she shuts down emotionally and then later gives me the silent treatment. She said, 'You didn't pray. You're reading books about goddesses and female religion. That's why you've forsaken the Lord.' To her I had turned against God.

"I said, 'I know it may seem that I've forsaken God, Mom, but that's not the case. I just can't be part of a religion that puts martyrdom on women and that has made you stay in a horrible marriage. I don't want that for my daughter.' She didn't say anything, but she was nodding yes, so I went on. 'I want my daughter to believe in a higher power. It doesn't really matter what that higher power is as long as she believes in something greater than herself that gives her strength—something that allows her to believe she can be whatever she wants to be, and something that doesn't make her forgo who she is in order to be happy.'

"My mom just looked at me and said nothing for the longest time, so I finished by saying, 'I hope you can understand because Gina [Alice's daughter] does. She does pray; she's just not given preauthorized prayer. She's allowed to make up whatever prayer that she wants. As well, I am very thankful for all the blessings I've had. I pray all the time. My prayers may not be like yours, but that doesn't make them any less.'

"Finally she spoke, 'I'm not happy, but I will accept what you're saying and I'm going to keep praying for your souls.'

"I knew that she was done talking about the issue, so we did what we always do: start talking about what my daughter and her cat were doing that day—a safe conversation for us to end our visit."

A few weeks later, Alice's mother sent her this letter:

Dear Alice,
   I'm so very proud of you. You're strong, and you stand by your beliefs. I admire how you're raising your daughter alone and that she's turned out to be who she is. You're a wonderful mother and daughter and she is a beautiful young woman.
   Love, Mom

Alice's success in connecting with her mother in spite of their differences was due in large part to the language Alice used to talk with her mother and her decision to forgo arguing and simply state her position, without being attached to the outcome.

The words Alice used to diffuse the tension with her mother can easily be adapted to any situation that involves a difference of opinion.

"You may be right." When your mother points out a difference, listen to her words, pause, and start your sentence with, "You may be right." Then add your own statement of what you believe. Transition with the word *and* (not *but*), and you will reduce her resistance.

"I know it may seem like . . ." Affirm her opinion or insight before you state your truth.

"I want my daughter . . ." Speak in *I* language. It is difficult for another person to hear you when you are blaming her (starting a sentence with the word *You* can sound like blaming). It is also harder for your mother to argue with your feelings when you make *I* statements.

"I hope you can understand . . ." Invite her to understand and state your ideal outcome.

"I'm grateful for . . ." Speak about what is helpful and working. Stay focused on the positive.

Broaden Your Horizons and Explore Your Mind-set

If you and your mother share the same spiritual path, you may attend the same church or temple, exchange Bible or Torah passages, or celebrate holidays in the same manner. Conversations about your faith are easy. You look forward to talking about how your life is enhanced by your spiritual practice. You have the chance to broaden your horizons. Ask yourself if there are new questions you could be asking. Are there new books you could be sharing, new lectures you could be going to with your mother, or volunteer activities the two of you could do together? There are many new and exciting ways to explore your faith, as well as revisiting the basics together.

If the two of you differ in your convictions regarding the divine, you know how challenging it can be to find common ground with such powerful and intimate thoughts. Perhaps you've moved away from the old family traditions while your mother has remained steadfast. Or maybe your mother has lost her faith as she's grown older, and you have found a new path that is deeply satisfying. You want to share this experience with her, but she's not interested. You may feel sad or indifferent that the two of you aren't closer. If your mother doesn't share your beliefs and you've given up talking with her about this topic, ask yourself the following question: Is it okay for the two of you to have different beliefs and still respect and enjoy each other? If not, why? If you're the one trying to convert her, understanding and accepting her perspective can be far more effective than convincing her that your way is a better way. If your mother is trying to convert you, can you honestly say that you have listened to her with open ears? Or have you tuned her out because you're tired of hearing the same old story? Have you told her what your beliefs are, or have you stayed silent to avoid a confrontation?

If your mother thinks you're trying to convert her, try this: "Mom, I'm not trying to convert you. While I would probably feel closer to you if you and I shared the same beliefs, I mostly want to understand what you do believe."

If your mother is trying to convert you, say this: "Mom, I understand how important your faith is to you. I wish I felt the same way as you do—and I don't. I think it's important that we talk about these things, but I need to be heard too. I'd like to tell you about my beliefs and why I believe what I do. Hopefully, this will help us better understand each other, and instead of an argument, open the door to a really interesting conversation."

Another way to diffuse the tension is to do exactly the opposite of what you usually do. If you normally throw up your hands and walk out of the room when she starts her sermon, instead take a deep breath and ask her to tell you more. She'll be surprised, you'll feel as if you've done your random act of kindness, and both of you will feel better.

Mom, How Do You Know It Was Heaven?

My mother made us promise we'd never tell anyone what she was about to tell us. We were at lunch with four of my friends for my thirty-third birthday. After saying our hellos, toasting with a glass of wine, and sharing small talk, Mom leaned into the table and said, "If my doctor or husband knew about this, they'd put me away for sure." Everyone leaned into the table and froze, waiting to hear what she was about to disclose.

She whispered, "When I was in the hospital and went into that coma from the bad blood they gave me, I went to heaven for a little while."

I felt a mixture of embarrassment and excitement. Had the wine gone to her head, or had she really had a near-death experience?

"Mom, how do you know it was heaven?" I asked.

She responded with such certainty that it took me by surprise. "Because I saw the beatific vision. I floated into a field out in the country and saw Jesus and Mother and Daddy, and the colors were brighter and more beautiful than anything I've ever seen on earth. The field was filled with shimmering flowers and green grass on a perfect summer day. Now you have to promise . . ."

" . . . not to tell anyone," I said, finishing her sentence and thinking about why she never told me about this apparition before. The faith of my mother's Catholic upbringing encompassed meeting Jesus after her death, not before. To speak of seeing Jesus while alive was considered blasphemous. I remember her telling me at too young an age that she had almost been committed to, as she called it, the sani-tearrrrrr-rium when I was a child. Her postpartum depression had been so bad that her doctor suggested shock treatments, which were never followed through on. Her memory of that experience was so strong that she feared having to deal with this happening again if she said the wrong thing. Not wanting to stir the pot, I kept my promise to keep her secret. From then on, whenever I thought about it, I felt a quiet smile creep across my face, knowing that my mother was far more spiritual than I ever gave her credit for.

Mom's revelation opened up a whole new channel of conversation and intimacy that I would never before have guessed possible. I felt more comfortable sharing more of my own intuitive experiences that didn't always make sense to me. She'd offer her insights, and we'd discuss these ideas the way I did with friends. We'd share dreams that each of us had and attempt to interpret them, often amused and amazed at what the other had experienced. I am so glad she took the risk to open herself that day to my friends and me. If she hadn't, I would have assumed that her religious beliefs would never have been able to encompass the broader spiritual experiences we'd both encountered privately. Her openness dramatically deepened our spiritual connection and stood us well at the end of her life.

Deepen Your Intuition and Your Intuitive Connection

If you've never spoken to your mother of spiritual experiences such as intuitive hunches you've had or dreams or visions that carry messages for you or others, here are two suggestions. Intuition expert Nancy Rosanoff, author of *Intuition Workout*, recommends that you say the following to your mother: "Mom, sometimes I get these feelings about what is going to happen or what decision I need to make, and I was wondering if you ever had experiences like that." If your mother says yes, encourage her to tell you about it by saying, "What happened?" or "I'd love to hear more about that." If she answers no, or even if she responds positively, also ask her, "Did your mother ever talk about her intuition?"

To encourage intuitive development in yourself and your mother (and daughters), she suggests that you continually ask before any big decision or any important event, "How do you feel about this?" The more you check out and validate your responses, the more active and helpful your intuition will be.

> *Intuition is a spiritual faculty and does not explain, but*
> *simply points the way.*
> —FLORENCE SCOVELL SHINN,
> *The Game of Life and How to Play It*

Prayer Works

Praying together is a marvelous way to deepen your connection to your mother, particularly if one of you is ill or in need of help. Kate, a health and fitness expert and mother of three boys, and her mother, Irene, not only pray together; they exchange prayer requests with names and photos of other people that they are praying for. Diana, a writer and television producer, didn't know what to say next during a heated argument with her mother about a traumatic family secret. Frustrated, she said to her mother, "I don't know what else to do. Maybe we should just pray together." Her mother (who is of a different religion) agreed, and the two of them prayed out loud, asking for insight and acceptance and more love in their relationship. When they finished praying, something shifted for her mother, and they experienced an unexpected breakthrough that resolved the issue.

Ask for Spiritual Guidance

Whether you're following a spiritual path that is traditional or of your own making, the time comes when the great beyond beckons. Having a strong sense of spirituality or religion and talking with your mother about her beliefs offers many rewards, but none so powerful as the peace that comes as your mother nears the end of her life. As my mother lay dying, knowing she had a belief that brought her comfort regarding her passing also gave me relief. It also helped that my aunt and uncles—Sister Francile, Brother Basil, and Father Dick—as well as the hospital chaplain—were regular visitors, always lifting my mother's spirits.

If you find yourself at the end of your mother's life and you're feeling lost, don't hesitate to talk to a spiritual counselor for guidance, whether that person is your minister, rabbi, or even your favorite psychic—or your mother's. These messengers can be extremely helpful in guiding you through this important passage.

I Think There's Something You Need to Say, and I Think You Need to Say It

Rabbi Lenore Bohm, mother of four and a woman I can always count on to deepen my spiritual awareness, remembers counseling the family of a woman dying of cancer. While sitting with the family in the hospital, Rabbi Bohm noticed that there was an unspoken tension in the room when everyone was present. She sensed that neither the mother nor her three daughters were ready to let go. Their holding on was causing the mother a lot of burdensome physical, emotional, and spiritual pain, which prevented the release she needed. The doctors said she had less than a week to live. She was bedridden and hadn't eaten in days. "I had the feeling," Rabbi Bohm recalled, "that if they were each able to say something to each other and get whatever they were holding back off their chests, they would be willing to let each other go.

"When I had been around the family socially before the mother got sick, there was a formality and practicality about her that made me think that she didn't share a lot of emotion with her daughters. Although I knew she was a devoted mother and raised them well, it was clear she loved them but also didn't say it a lot and wasn't a tender mother with them."

Ask and you shall receive, seek and you shall find, knock and it shall be opened to you.

—LUKE 11:9

"I asked the daughters to leave the room. As I sat quietly with this mother, I said to her, 'What do you want them to know? What is it you want to tell them? If you don't want to tell them, I can tell them. I can tell them after you die, if you prefer, but I think there's something you need to say and that you're not saying it. I think it's preventing your release here.' It was really very bold of me and I'm not sure where it came from. I was really pushing her, and everyone else was treating her so gently. I urged her one last time: 'I think there's something you need to say, and I think you need to say it.'

"The mother said, 'I love my daughters deeply and I am concerned about their well-being. I want them to look after each other and take care of each other.' And then the kicker came. She said that she felt badly she hadn't told her daughters often enough or showed them enough how much she really did love them and that she didn't want to leave without having said that.

"I went out to the girls and said, 'I want you all to know that it's very important your mother know that you understand how much she loved you. If in any way she wasn't forthcoming with that love, it had nothing to do with the quality of it. It had to do with her personality and her generation.' They all understood what I was saying. Interestingly, they all were carrying a similar burden, saying, 'We didn't tell her enough that we loved her. We didn't show her enough that we loved her.' I said, 'Maybe all of you should be together now and have this exchange of love and begin to move on to the next place without fear.' They did exchange these sentiments with a lot of tears and hugging, and the mother died peacefully that night."

When Rabbi Bohm related this story to me, I found myself nodding. First of all, Rabbi Bohm's gift of presence transformed and helped a mother pass away in harmony and completeness. Second, it reconfirmed my belief that all of life is a prayer for love. If you haven't said, "I love you" to your mother lately, don't wait. Pick up the phone right now, and tell her, even if she's never said, "I love you" to you. A few simple words of direction and encouragement, along with an intention of understanding, can release even the most stubborn of people to rise to their moments of spiritual greatness. All of these actions can be summed up in one word: *love.* God is love. You are love. Your mother is love. In the beginning and in the end, all there is is love.

Divine Love melts all situations that seem impossible.
—CATHERINE PONDER,
Prospering Power of Love

Activities to Do with Your Mom

❑ Pray together.
❑ Walk in nature.
❑ Go on a cruise that offers spiritual workshops. For information, see http.//www.theinnervoyage.com.
❑ Form a women's group or mother-daughter group for chanting, devotional singing, Bible study, or meditation.
❑ Attend religious services together, and then share a meal.
❑ Write each other letters of inspiration describing favorite spiritual passages and ways that you strengthen your faith.
❑ Take a yoga class.

Questions to Ask Your Mom

• Do you believe in God? If so, how do you envision God? Heaven? Hell?
• Did you have a specific experience where you learned there was a God, or have you always believed and never questioned?
• When or where do you feel most connected to a higher power?
• Where do you turn when you are unable to make sense of tragedy or loss?

- What is one of the most mystical or spiritual experiences you've had?
- Where do you feel most connected in your life?
- Have you had an experience that tested your faith? Confirmed your faith?
- What are some of your favorite prayers? Spiritual passages? Songs?
- What is your favorite religious holiday?
- Have you ever been to a psychic? What would convince you to go?
- Have you ever had your astrological chart done? Do you believe it helps?
- Have you ever witnessed a miracle? What happened?
- What intuitive hunches have you had that you're glad you followed?
- If you were God for a day, what would you do with the world?
- What do you think happens after death?

CONVERSATION 9

The Rose

Death and Dying

Remember my friend Fran from Conversation 2? The woman whose finances were so well organized that her daughter, Lori, would know exactly what to do if Fran died? The woman who said to me after my mother died, "I know you'll never be able to replace your mother, but if you need a second mom, I'm here for you"? The woman whose motto was "I'm a tough old bird"? She died last Wednesday morning. Suddenly. A blood clot in her lung.

It's still hard to believe. It wasn't supposed to happen. Mothers aren't supposed to die. They're supposed to be there for us whenever we need them. They're supposed to live forever. And when they don't, no matter how much closeness or distance there has been between us, there's always something we wish we had asked or said before they passed away.

Your ability to talk with your mother about death will be one of the single most important things that you do for both of you. Having witnessed my own mother's passing and having talked with hundreds of women over the past nine years whose mothers have also died, I promise you that your life will be different after using the techniques and asking the questions suggested in this topic.

If you're feeling uneasy about doing, this, I completely understand. It isn't easy. Do it anyway. Of all the conversations you will have with your mother, this one has the potential to be very uncomfortable, as well as very enlightening, healing, and comforting. At times, your heart will ache, and more than likely you will fight back tears, if not outright cry, as will your mother. But you will also find yourself lighter and better prepared to deal with the inevitable. Loss is a difficult experience to resolve. Loss is lonely. But loss is also freeing. The sooner you have this conversation, the better prepared you will be to continue living. You will never be completely prepared for the experience, but if your mother should die suddenly, you will know what to do. If your mother has a lingering illness, you will know what to do. And when she needs you most and is least likely to ask for help, you will know what to do.

Every word in this book prior to this topic has been written to help you prepare for this conversation. If you still have unexpressed hurts, now is the time to address them so they don't keep you from being as loving as you want to be when you do talk with your mom about death.

What Does Death Mean to You?

Before talking with your mother, write a few pages in your journal about your own views and experiences of death. Grief therapist Alexandra Kennedy, author of *Losing a Parent*, suggests answering these questions:

- What does death mean to you? Finality? Immortality? Relief? Fear? Reunion with God? Peace and quiet?
- How do you feel about your own death?
- What experiences have you had with death? Have they been traumatic? Frightening? Not talked about? A natural part of life?
- What brushes with death have you had, if any? A car accident? Childhood illness? Cancer? Thoughts of suicide?
- What is most important for you to say to your mother about death? Do you need to resolve unfinished business? Talk to her about your own fears? Tell her how grateful you are for her nurturing and encouragement?

Take your time answering these questions, because they will lead you into a world that has the potential to deepen your intimacy with your mother beyond anything else you've experienced. Not only will you be clearer about your own thoughts, but also when you speak with your mother, if she turns the questions back at you, your answers will give her strength and encouragement to keep talking.

Timing Is Important

Once you have identified your own values, beliefs, and attitudes about death, it's time to talk with your mother. The timing of this conversation is very important. You want your mother to be receptive to what you have to say. If she's healthy, choose a place where the two of you can talk freely—perhaps a walk or a drive home after church or temple services. If she's ill or immobile, choose a time of day when she isn't tired, or just after she's had her medication and is stable. Don't push the subject. If she's not ready to talk, forcing the issue will only push her away. If you are sensitive to her needs as well as your own, a space will open for you to address your concerns and ask her questions. While she may not choose to answer you, if you speak from your heart using I-focused language, she will be more likely to listen to you, and you will keep the door open for a future conversation.

How Do I Get Started?

How do you talk to your mom about death? Thoughtfully. Directly. Deeply. Lightheartedly. Whatever way feels most like you at your best and will help your mother open up. Most important, make sure to have the talk. It's not pleasant to think about, but your mother could be taken away from you at any time, and the loss you will feel is as deep as the ocean.

Ease into Your Conversation

There are many opportunities to initiate discussion, not all of them necessarily focused on her death. Women live an average of eight to ten years longer than men, so if your father or your mother's husband is still alive, talking with her about his death can ease you into a conversation about her death.

Consider these additional situations that support a discussion on death and dying:

- Driving past a funeral
- Reading about a tragic death in the newspaper
- After watching a movie, video, television show, or news program dealing with death
- The birthday, death, or death anniversary of your mother's parents
- The death or illness of another family member or friend
- Your own mother's illness

Every mother is different in how she will respond to the topic of death and dying. Some mothers want to talk about and control every detail down to the specific flower arrangement that will be laid on the casket and in what key the vocalist should sing *Ave Maria*, while others turn their head when they see a funeral procession and won't even allow the word *death* mentioned around them. Most conversations about death in families today are indirect. One sister talks to another sister about what to do with Mom, but neither talks directly with her. Mom tells her doctor she's afraid to die but never mentions it to her daughter. While there has been some shift due to the growth of the hospice movement, our culture still does not support straightforward conversations about one's mortality. Is it a surprise that we still tend to avoid, downplay, or sugarcoat the dying process?

Some women I talked with said it was they who were more uncomfortable talking about death than their mothers. Their mothers brought up death during their own illness—some conversations covert, others overt. Tevyan, a daughter I interviewed for the chapter on conflict, had been distant from her mother until the day Tevyan's sister, Cindi, died of breast cancer three years ago. After telling her mother, Johnnie Bea, who was also recently diagnosed with cancer, "Daddy's gone. Cindi's gone. You can't die. I need you," the two women had a breakthrough. A friendship developed, and they have been in daily contact ever since.

In the past six months, Johnnie Bea's health has been deteriorating rapidly. A few weeks ago after finding her mother in agonizing pain, Tevyan rushed her to the hospital. "In the emergency room," Tevyan recalled, "my mom said, 'You know I'm tired. Will you be okay?' I knew exactly what she was saying, and I said back to her, 'I know you're tired. And I'll be okay.' We never talked directly about her dying, but I knew that's what she meant. My sister-in-law told me that when she took my mom back to her oncologist a few weeks later, he asked if she'd made peace with someone she loved because she was so relaxed. My mom said, 'Yes, my Baby (that's what she calls me) says that if I die, she can deal with it; she'll be okay.' Don't get me wrong, I do need her, and I'll always need her. She's my mom. I have a friend in her I never had before. I'll miss that. But I don't want her to hurt. I have enough peace with her, and she's ready to go."

Use Your Intuition to Decipher Her Unspoken Messages

Some mothers on an intuitive level know they are going to die, and although they may not directly discuss their death, their actions around possessions and activities change. It is up to their daughters to decipher the message they are sending and respond appropriately. Jane, a software specialist, thought it was odd that her mother, who was healthy and in her late sixties, started passing on family heirlooms and telling her three daughters who would get the china, the crystal, and the silver. Six months later, her mother, who was in good health, died unexpectedly of a stroke. Alexandra Kennedy spoke of a young woman named Pam who came to her "Losing a Parent" workshop at the request of her mother. Pam said, "I'm doing this for my mother. She's so worried I won't be able to cope if she should die, even though she's really healthy. She thinks this will prepare me." That evening after the workshop, Pam went to her mother's for dinner and told her mother how much she learned. The two talked about death and had a conversation Pam never would have initiated. That night, Pam's mother died in her sleep of a heart attack.

If you are the one who avoids the issue of death, when your mother brings it up, let your mother's strength support you. When her time comes, you will find great solace in being able to respond to her need to talk about her death. Nanci, in her fifties says, "I can't imagine what I'll do when I lose my mother. Just thinking about her death brings tears.

When I tell her that, she says in her quiet matter-of-fact way, 'Well, I know but someday I'm going to have to leave.' "

> *I don't want to die. I think death is a greatly over-rated experience.*
>
> —RITA MAE BROWN, *Bingo*

What do you do if your mother is faced with a sudden crisis, and her life is at risk? Fran's health crisis, unexpected death, and the circumstances her daughter, Lori, had to deal with throughout this time serve as a clear reminder of how important it is to know what your mother's wishes and needs are regarding the final days of her life. You want to be able to be a caregiver to her during her crisis and to yourself when she dies.

Fran, in her early seventies, was in good health. She and Lori, in her mid-thirties, had a very close relationship, seeing each other several days a week. When Lori's sister, Diane, was diagnosed with ovarian cancer three years ago at age forty-eight, Lori and Fran alternated caring for her at their homes for eighteen months until Diane's death.

Eighteen months after Diane died, Fran called 911 at midnight because her heart was racing and her blood pressure had shot up beyond a safe level. Not wanting to wake Lori, whose husband was out of town on business and whose baby was finally sleeping through the night, Fran waited until the next morning to call her. After Fran's doctor ruled out heart disease, cancer, and lupus, she was released two days later with a diagnosis of anemia. Lori brought Fran home, only to end up rushing her back to the hospital the next morning when she collapsed in her bathroom. Her doctor was unable to determine what caused Fran's collapse and decided to watch her for twenty-four hours. He reassured Lori that while Fran's condition was perplexing, she was not in a life-or-death situation. Lori called her brother, John (my partner), and me that afternoon to tell us what happened.

Upon hearing the news, I called Fran immediately. She sounded breathy and anxious. As I listened to her talk, an unsettling question went through my mind, which I could not brush off. Fearing that I'd sound insensitive but trusting my intuition, I hesitantly asked, "Fran, are you afraid you're going to die?" "Yes," she said. "I need Johnny. I have things to tell him." I assured her that he'd be there as quickly as possible. We exchanged "I love yous" and ended our call.

Confused by the contrast between Fran's fear that she was dying and the doctor's earlier assurance that all was okay, I called the hospital for more information. The doctor was unavailable, but the nurse manager said Fran's vital signs were strong and Fran was likely just frightened. She reassured me that Fran's knowing about our planned arrival on Saturday (she lived in Michigan, we live in San Diego), four days later, would calm her down. In the evening, Lori called us again saying Fran was resting comfortably.

Eight hours later, at six o'clock in the morning, Lori got a call from the hospital telling her to come quickly. Having slept at her mother's in case Fran needed anything from home, Lori dressed quickly, took her infant son to the next-door neighbor, and rushed to the hospital ten minutes away. When she arrived, she was told her mother had died fifteen minutes earlier from a blood clot that went to her lung. Alone and in shock, Lori drove to her own home to find four phone messages that were left between four and five o'clock in the morning from the hospital urging her to come quickly. The hospital staff didn't know Lori was at her mother's house until one nurse thought to call Fran's house as a last resort.

As Lori recalled her experience, she said, "I can't believe this happened. I never got to say good-bye. I've lost my mother and my best friend."

Lori's experience serves as a powerful reminder that even the best intentions cannot always prevent a crisis. The key is being prepared. Here are six rules to remember should your mother ever face a life-or-death situation.

Rule 1. Let your mother know how important it is for her to contact you immediately if she is in a real or imagined life-or-death situation. No matter what time of day or night it is. No matter where you are on the planet. It is not in most mothers' natures to ask for help from their children. Your mother needs to hear directly from you that she can count on you in an emergency.

Rule 2. If your mother argues with you against taking emergency action that you feel she needs, overrule her. It is better to be safe than sorry. You can always resolve anger, but you can't bring your mother back from the dead. Be clear. Be direct. Be strong. Sometimes even your mother wants and needs direction but doesn't know how to ask for it. A simple, direct comment that guides her will keep both of you calm: "Mom, I know this is difficult for you, but we both want the same thing: for you to be healthy and safe. Please do as I ask."

Rule 3. Ask for help from your other family members. Family caregivers are typically daughters in their forties who are also raising children and working outside the home. This is not a time to try and do everything yourself. You must be as assertive about your needs as you are about your mother's care.

Rule 4. Trust your intuition, and speak up. If you are dealing with a life-threatening situation, you may save your mother's life or ease her death. If your mother is offended by the question, "Are you afraid you're going to die?" she will survive, and she always has the choice to respond, "No, I'm not afraid!" If she is genuinely frightened or needs to talk and doesn't know how to start, you're opening a window for her. Hospice experts will tell you that people often know when they're close to death, especially if they're extremely ill or elderly, but everyone else dismisses it because they were afraid to ask the question, "Is death near?" for fear of being rude, or their own grief prevented them.

Rule 5. Triple-check locations and phone numbers with medical staff before you leave the hospital. Don't depend only on the chart information or original paperwork to identify your location. Leave written notes taped to the phone and near the door of her hospital room stating "In an emergency, call . . ."

Rule 6. When saying your daily good-byes on the phone or in person, especially as your mother becomes frailer or if she is ill, act as if they were your last. A Zen prayer suggests that we always carry death on our shoulder because it reminds us to appreciate the life that is before us in the moment.

No one expects their mother to die. Whether she dies suddenly or has been ill for a long time, the silence after her last breath is still shocking, her spirit a mystery. Our work is to make friends with the mystery, and one of the best ways to do that is to make friends with the impending death of our mother.

Preplan Your Mother's Funeral with Her

There are several ways to prepare yourself and your mother for either of your deaths. Planning the funerals of my parents, participating in the planning of Fran's, and attending more than I ever care to go to hasn't been fun, but it has been important, meaningful, and helpful. It's very clear to me that preplanning funerals with our loved ones would help us all. Making funeral decisions for someone you have loved and lost is unsettling, surreal, and emotional. What should I bury her in? Would she have liked that prayer said? Which casket is best? Ironically, some states have a law that says even if your mother's will spells out her funeral service, with the exception of donating her body to science, your wishes as her next of kin supersede hers. Knowing what is coming and what to do makes the process more bearable when it does happen.

Here are some suggestions to help make your mother's death easier for both of you:

- Focus on celebrating your mother's life. Consider having a celebration-of-life party on a birthday that would otherwise slip by. Have people bring stories, poems, and songs to share that best represent their experience of your mother.
- Help each other write what you would want written in your obituaries.

- Ask your mother to write a "legacy letter" that can be read to her loved ones at her service, telling them what she wants people to remember about her and moving forward in life.
- Check your mother's insurance policies (and your own) to see what kind of death benefits are included. Some life insurance companies cover funeral expenses up to a certain amount. If not, you can purchase a policy that will cover just the funeral. In those early moments of grief just after your mother has died, deciding how much you can or want to spend on her funeral is the last thing you want to be thinking about, but it will be the first thing you'll need to know. Today's funeral costs an average of $5,000 to $10,000.
- Plan her funeral (and yours) with her before you need to do so. Visit a funeral home, and ask the director to walk you through all the steps of a funeral. Write your mom's plan down, and have her transfer it to a living will. Does she want an open casket or a cremation and memorial service? At the funeral home? Church? Her home? A park? If she wants to be buried, what outfit does she want to be wearing? If she'll be cremated, how does she want her ashes dispersed? If you're having a service, what music does she want played? What stories and songs does she want told and sung? How does she want people to remember her?

The Suitcase Under the Bed

When I was talking to Fran and Lori about their relationship six months ago, Fran recalled that when her mother, Manuela, developed peritonitis at eighty-four, she knew she was dying. Manuela told a surprised Fran that her funeral dress was in the suitcase underneath her bed with the deed to the house. "Sure enough, my sister and I found the suitcase with a peachy chiffon evening gown, gold evening slippers, and the sheerest nylons you've ever seen. We had never seen the dress until that day. I guess Momma was planning to dance her way to heaven. We weren't sure how they would get her into the dress until we took it out of the suitcase. We laughed so hard when we noticed that there was a zipper all the way to the bottom (the zipper was actually a slipcover zipper from a sofa), so that when rigor mortis set in, they'd still be able to get the dress on. She thought of everything. My sister didn't know a thing about it and wondered how I knew, given that she was the one who lived around the block from Momma. I don't think she thought to ask."

Am I Going to Die?

The idea of thinking to ask a question becomes the key that determines how much intimacy we are able to create, the lessons we will learn, and the love we will carry with us after our mother is gone.

I had two conversations with my mother about death. The first conversation came unexpectedly one morning a year and a half before she died. My father called me at ten o'clock in the morning at work, which he never did. His normally booming voice was shaky and sounded panicky. Words rushed out of his mouth, "Mary, come quickly. Something's wrong with your mother, and I don't know what to do." I left work and sped over to their house ten minutes away, wondering what I would encounter. When I got there, my father was pacing in the kitchen, and my mother was lying on the double bed in the guest room with eyes rolled backward, moaning in pain, and every bodily fluid releasing itself. I had never seen her like this and cried out, "Dad, call the doctor. Mom, can you hear me?" Her voice was filled with fear when she said, "Mary, is that you?"

"Yes, Mom."

"Oh, Mary, I'm so scared. I hurt so much. Am I going to die?"

I froze, not knowing what to say. I prayed like I've never prayed before and begged God to help my mother and give me words to answer her question. Imagine if your mother asked you that question. How would you respond? As I stood there, I heard a voice in my head say, "What would your mother say to you?" On automatic pilot, I took my mother's hand and said, "Mom, I don't know if you're going to die, but if you need to, it's okay. I love you." And in that moment as she squeezed my hand, I remembered that when I was a little girl and hurt myself, she would take my hand and say, "When it hurts, Mary, squeeze my hand, and I'll tell you that I love you." I looked at her lying there and gently squeezed her hand back and said, "Mom, when it hurts, squeeze my hand, and I'll tell you that I love you."

Minutes passed while I held her hand, waiting for a response from her and from the doctor. Miraculously, she opened her eyes and said, "I love you too. I'm feeling better." Within an hour it was as if nothing happened to her. The doctor said she probably had a severe case of the flu. We didn't know it at the time, but that episode was one of her early warning signs for ovarian cancer.

Mom reminded me over and over throughout her illness how grateful she was for those words of comfort. I learned a powerful lesson that day: when you don't know what to say, don't fight for words. Simply get quiet, and trust that your intuition will give you the words you need to say. This awareness has never failed me.

Mom, How Do You Feel About Dying?

We assume that we know our mother doesn't want to die, *and* that it will be horrible for her, *and* how dare we even talk about death since she's still alive. Even if all three statements were true, we miss a tremendous opportunity to open a deep well of potential insight and healing by assuming we know what our mother is thinking. It is often our own fear of the topic of death that keeps us from asking our mother how she feels about dying.

The second time I broached the subject of death with Mom was the night she was featured on the evening news. She had agreed to take an experimental drug that had the potential—if it worked—to lengthen an ovarian cancer patient's life. If the drug didn't work, it could kill her. The reporter asked her, "Grace, why did you do this dangerous experimental procedure?" In a weak voice she said, "Because I want to help other women so they don't have to go through what I did." As I watched her, I broke down in tears. Here she was full of cancer, drugs, and tremendous pain, and she was more concerned about helping other women than she was about herself. That was the night the inevitability of her death and my loss really hit me.

After everyone had left her room and we were alone, I kept wondering how she felt about coming to the end of her life. I knew I would be mad and scared if it were happening to me. I wanted to ask her, but I felt unsure if it was appropriate. I wished I had a Miss Manners Guide to Death. I must have rehearsed my words a hundred times in my head, and finally in a moment of silence, I said, "Mom how do you feel about dying?" She said, "I don't want to talk about it now. I just want to live." It was rare that Mom didn't want to talk. I was taken aback and not sure what to say next but trusted that the right words would come if I got quiet. I paused and the next words out of my mouth were, "Okay, but let's make a pact. If there is life after death, find a way to contact me. But don't scare me. Just turn the light on or off, or do something that will get my attention." She laughed and said, "What if you go before I do? I'll agree if you agree." First I was shocked; I hadn't consciously contemplated my own death. Then I laughed as I recognized once again her simple way of reminding me that life doesn't always go the way you expect it to and to lighten up and enjoy the moment.

"Okay," I said, "so if there is life on the other side, whoever goes first will contact the one left behind without scaring them."

"Fine," she said, "but if you decide to turn on the lights for me, remember to turn them off before you float out of the room. You know how your father hates it when anyone leaves the lights on."

I was lucky in that I had five months with my mother to prepare for her death. Even then, I still wasn't ready to let her go or consider my own death, but at least there was time to find ways to bring closure to our life together. Three years later, my own cervical cancer scare and subsequent hysterectomy pushed that mysterious door of death wide open. I realized how important it is, like it or not, to talk about issues of death and dying with those you love before it's too late. Choosing to put myself in a curious frame of mind seems to ease my fear. It's still not easy for me, but I have become more willing to ask questions, which has led to answers that astound me, teach me, and comfort me.

Every Mother Has Her Life Wisdom

What if your mother is within days or hours of death? What do you do then? Sometimes we don't know what to say. In those moments, instead of trying to fill the space with words, try silence. Sogyal Rinpoche, author of *The Tibetan Book of Living and Dying*, suggests sitting and holding your mother's hand and letting her talk. He writes, "I have been amazed again and again by how, if you just let people talk, giving them your complete and compassionate attention, they will say things of a surprising spiritual depth, even when they think they don't have any spiritual beliefs. Everyone has his or her own life wisdom, and when you let a person talk you allow this life wisdom to emerge."

Therapist and former hospice social worker Mary Rice suggests playing your mother's favorite music in the background as you sit with her. "Music speaks to the soul. When there are no words to speak, music will say all that you need to say and all your mother needs to hear. And oftentimes creates a path for both of you to speak from your heart." Mary spoke of a client in the midst of grieving the imminent loss of her mother, who was dying of cancer. In the last days of her life, the daughter played her mother's favorite Big Band music. Her mother said she felt less pain while the music was playing. As well, the music brought back some of her favorite memories of when she and her husband were newlyweds and danced together.

What legacy does your mother want to leave you? Her family? The world? You can enrich your mother's final moments by asking her about the highlights of her life, the times that filled her with joy, the memories that mean the most to her. One of the greatest gifts we give another person at the end of life is to ask about memories of love, joy, and pleasure. Help your mother relive those moments. Ask her what has made her happy, what trips and people and experiences were memorable to her. And when you are faced with her passing, should you be fortunate enough to be with her in the last moments of her life, wish her well, and give thanks for all that she has given you. Without your mother, where would you be?

It's Okay to Let Go

Mom entered a coma two weeks before she died. Not aware that it was her last night of consciousness, I held her hand and yelled into her ear (remember, she was hard of hearing), "I love you, Mom!" Her voice was too weak to carry sound, but she squeezed my hand and, through parched lips, mouthed her last words to me, "I love you."

After a week, our hospice nurse encouraged us to continue talking with Mom, reassuring her that we loved her. She noticed Mom was having a difficult time letting go and said, "Sometimes gentle words of encouragement such as, 'It's okay to let go. We love you,' can make it easier for people." My mother's faith was unshakable, and her belief that she would be reunited with her parents and Jesus gave her great peace and comfort even when she was in tremendous pain. The night before she died, I overheard my sister Eileen say to her, "Mom, it's okay to let go. You'll be with Jesus, and you'll be able to shop forever. You'll like that."

> *Her presence influenced who I was, and her absence*
> *influences who I am. Our lives are shaped as much by those*
> *who leave us as they are by those who stay. Loss is our legacy.*
> *Insight is our gift. Memory is our guide.*
> —HOPE EDELMAN, *Motherless Daughters*

Activities to Do with Your Mom

- ❑ Take a grief workshop together before you need it.
- ❑ Volunteer at a hospice together (this can be daunting, but equally enlightening).
- ❑ Go to a funeral home together (before illness or accident happens), and walk through all the steps with a funeral director.
- ❑ Help each other write a eulogy and an obituary of at least 250

words, including your interests and what was most important to you.

❑ Watch the film *One True Thing*, the story of how a family—in particular, a twenty-something daughter—deals with the impending death of the mother. The original story with the same title by Anna Quindlen (whose mother died of cancer when Anna was seventeen) is available in bookstores.

Questions to Ask Your Mom

- What was your first experience of death?
- Have you ever been with someone who died? Who? What happened?
- What do you think happens after death?
- If you have a medical emergency that might render you totally incapacitated, do you want to be resuscitated? What situation might be the exception? Have you written your wishes down in a living will?
- How do you feel about a nursing home? Hospice care?
- Are you interested in being an organ donor?
- Who would you like with you at your death?
- Do you have a will? Living will? Living trust? Where are the papers? Who is the executor?
- Please tell me what you would like me to do regarding your funeral arrangements. Do you want your body to be buried or cremated? Do you want an open or closed casket? If you are cremated, how would you like your ashes to be dispersed?
- What clothing do you want to be buried in?
- What kind of service do you want? Do you want visitation at a funeral home? A celebration-of-life service at home? A church service? Graveside service?
- What prayers, poems, or stories would you like read? Music played and songs sung? By whom?
- Is there anything you don't want me to do regarding your funeral plans?

- Do you have a burial plot? Do you want a grave marker? What do you want the marker to say?
- What comments would you like in your obituary?
- Will you write me a letter telling me what's been important to you in your life so that I can read it after you're gone?

Wind Beneath My Wings

Appreciation

More than 150 million greeting cards are exchanged every Mother's Day. It's the number one gift given to mothers, followed by flowers, plants, clothing, and jewelry. All the major long-distance companies say Mother's Day is their busiest day of the year. They log 130 million calls compared to a normal Sunday of 90 million. When the U.S. Postal Service did a poll last year, 62 percent of the survey group said they normally visit their mom on Mother's Day.

Think about all the different ways you've appreciated your mother over the years. What kind of gifts have you given her? Preprinted cards? Flowers? Candy? Jewelry? Clothing? I'm sure your mother enjoyed them, but have you ever wondered what she'd buy herself under the same circumstances? In a recent national retailers' poll of mothers, 49 percent of mothers expected flowers; 13 percent said they wanted them. It's presence, not presents, that counts. All of the mothers I interviewed said the flowers and candy and other material gifts were nice, but the gift of spending time with them had the most lasting memory. There were four types of appreciation mothers said they wanted most:

- Time
- Kindness in words and actions
- Captured memories
- Services that improve the quality of her life

The Time Is Now

Time has a very different meaning for our mothers than it does for us. You can put off doing what you don't have time for now and know you'll eventually do it later. Not so with your mother. Her measurement of time is much shorter, so there is more urgency for her to spend time with you now. Even if you can't give her all the time she wants, make the time you have with her count. As the time with my own mother grew shorter, I found myself begging God to turn back the clock. I lamented all the times I multi-tasked when I was with her. I'd flip through the paper or a magazine while she talked. If she phoned me, I'd open bills, cook, wash dishes—anything to feel I was being productive. If I had it to do over again, honestly, I know I'd still do some of that, but I'd save fifteen minutes just for her, with no distractions. I'd listen with my full attention. I'd ask questions of interest instead of interrogating her, and I'd give her much more empathy. I've learned an amazing thing about communication: when you are truly present with a person in thoughts and body, whatever you are attempting to accomplish—relaying information, persuading, complaining, empathizing—is done more efficiently and pleasurably. If you become fidgety or bored when talking with your mom, ask yourself how engaged with her you are. Start asking more questions, or being more attentive to the conversation. Use gentler words. Be more honest. Talk about happy memories more often.

Each day we're given the same twenty-four hours to live our life. How much time is in your schedule to appreciate your mother? If you haven't talked to your mom in the past few days, go to the phone right now and give her the gift of your voice and your time. Tell her one reason why you love her. Then come back and finish the chapter.

> If the only prayer you said in your whole life was, "Thank
> you," that would suffice.
> —MEISTER ECKHART, in *Gratitude: A Field
> Notebook for Thoughts and Reflections*

That's So Lovely. I Wish She Would Tell Me That.

So often we think we have to provide Mom with expensive gifts or top ourselves from the year before. Or we spend more time looking for her gift than we do talking to her. Or we tell our friends how great our mother is, but we forget to tell her.

The other day I called a friend's mother to find out how she felt when she received a particularly wonderful gift from my friend and her children. She remarked, "Oh, I cried and cried. I was so touched. I look at it every day." I then went on to say, "I am so glad I'm getting to know you better. Your daughter thinks the world of you—she said to me, 'I really respect my mother. I wouldn't dismiss her perspective on ideas or people about which we differ, because she's a really smart woman and she thinks deeply about things. She's always encouraged me to think for myself. She's always made me feel I could do anything. She saw mothering as a profession and took it very seriously. A huge part of my success is because of my mother." There was a long pause on the phone, and then my friend's mother said, "That's so lovely. I wish she would tell me that."

Why is it that the very thing that we say is most important in life—giving and receiving love—is so often overlooked, dismissed, withheld, and denied? My audiences tell me they don't give praise because "It's too embarrassing," or "They'll get a big head," or "I just didn't think to do it." Do it anyway! Researchers at the HeartMath Institute in Colorado have proven that appreciation not only lifts people's spirits, it also improves the immune system, relaxes the nervous system, and regulates heart rhythm.

Six Tips for Perfect Praise

One of the most meaningful and least expensive ways to appreciate your mother is simply to tell her what you value about her. Give her a compliment. Here are six tips to help you acknowledge your mother more easily:

Tip 1. Catch her in the act of being herself at her best, doing something good, honorable, kind, or helpful. Research done by Blanchard Training and Development has shown that we need twelve positive comments to overcome one negative. Dr. John

Gottman, coauthor with Nan Silver of *The Seven Principles for Making Marriage Work*, found in his research that the common denominator in successful marriages is five positive gestures or statements for every one criticism. The bottom line is that everyone needs positive feedback. Check in with yourself. How often do you acknowledge your mother? Make a list of ten of her strengths, talents, and skills. Write them down on a card, and read them to her. Tell her that the rules are that there is no playing down or denying that what you say is true and that if she can't think of anything to say, "Thank you" is enough.

Tip 2. Be specific in what you're praising. Instead of saying, "Thanks for calling, Mom," say, "Thanks Mom, for asking how my meeting went. You always remember the details of my life. I feel so loved by you."

Tip 3. Use positive words. When Peggy Noonan was writing speeches for President Ronald Reagan, she changed his words from "I'll never forget you" to "I'll always remember you." It may seem like a small detail, but changing your language from negative to positive can make a difference in your level of energy and how people respond to you. Our energy decreases when we use negative words and increases when we hear and say positive words.

Tip 4. Be immediate with your praise. People don't change without a sense of urgency. If you want to change your thoughts about your mother from criticism to appreciation, you'll want to acknowledge her positive actions as quickly as possible. Do this for yourself, too. Give yourself praise throughout the day, and you'll be less dependent on your mother's praise to validate you.

Tip 5. Be sincere. Remember the time you flattered someone because you felt the person needed to hear it, and the response was one of surprise or denial. Perhaps it was because your intent was to make her feel better rather than to acknowledge honestly something positive you noticed. It is essential to tell the truth. Rather than flatter or patronize your mother, acknowledge that she seems a little down and ask, "What can I do to help?"

Tip 6. Be personal. Acknowledge how you feel about what your mother did for you. Positive feelings such as happiness, satisfaction, gratitude, pride, pleasure, relaxation, relief, joy, confidence, and competence motivate us to be better. "Thank you so much for offering to drive me to the doctor. I've been scared about this appointment, and having you there will help keep me calm."

Capture Memories in a Memory Jar

After running out of ideas and giving her mother too many fruitcakes, Mary LoVerde, author of *Stop Screaming at the Microwave,* created a "memory jar" for her mother for Mother's Day one year. She wrote out one hundred memories on single slips of paper, starting with the words, "I remember . . ."—"I remember our talk the night before I got married," "I remember calling you from the hospital and telling you your first grandchild had been born." After rolling up each slip of paper, she dropped them into a crystal jar with a lid and included the following letter.

> *Dear Mom,*
> *I'm busy. I know I neglect you. But I want you to know that what you did for me made a happy and healthy person. I love you and think of you every day. Please read these memories and think of me.*
> *Love, Mary*

Mary recalls that she told her mother to read one memory a day, but her mother had finished all of them before the end of the first day and kept rereading them. Give your mother a memory jar for her next birthday or Mother's Day or when she's not feeling well. You'll lift her spirit and remind her how much she is loved.

Create a Memory Album and Video

For her mother's eightieth birthday, Mary Jane Mapes, a communications consultant and speaker, and the mother of two young adults, organized a four-part celebration that involved her mother Mabel's entire family and all her friends. The first part was a memory album. Forty-three family members including nine children received their own two-page layout. On the left page was a heart filled in with a special memory each person had of Mabel and on the right were various pictures of themselves.

The second part was a video that included photos dating back as far as Mabel's parents' wedding and included her own birth, childhood, school days, marriage, and family life. Accompanying the photos was music that matched the era that the pictures represented. This was followed by three-minute testimonials spoken by each of her nine children, telling Mabel directly why they were grateful for her in their lives. They completed the video with rolling movie credits, including the names of all the family members.

The third part of the celebration involved ninety friends of Mabel. Mary Jane explains, "We sent a letter to all her friends, telling them that we were having a card party. We asked that they send her a birthday card and include a special memory or picture. Everyone sent something."

The final piece of the jubilation was a birthday party attended by everyone who contributed to the project. Mary Jane explains, "At this point in my mother's life, all she really needs from us is our love and gratitude and devotion. With so much opportunity for many women today, and with two accomplished daughters, I know that my mother has had moments of doubt as to whether her life as a homemaker and mother was really as significant as it might have been had she made other choices. Well, on my mother's eightieth birthday, not one person in the room would have told you that there could be anything more significant than bringing nine children into the world and being a mother who exemplified unconditional love, a servant's heart, and unwavering faith in God. If you could have heard the individual videos, you would have heard this message repeated over and over again."

What a tribute! And how wonderful to be able to do this while her mother was still alive and could enjoy it. What will you do to celebrate your mother this year?

Give Services That Improve the Quality of Life

As your mother grows older, she may not have the strength or the extra income to afford services that could help make her life easier such as meal services, newspaper delivery, or lawn mowing. Your involvement can relieve her of worry and improve the quality of her life. Chris gave her mother a snowplowing service for Christmas this year. Lorna treated her mother to a day at the spa, with a massage, manicure, and pedicure for her birthday. Susan took her mother to lunch for Mother's Day and surprised her with a weekly grocery shopping delivery service. Anne offered to wash her mother's floors once a month.

Know What Motivates Your Mother

Have you ever received a gift from your mother (or anyone else) that you never would have wanted in a million years? Every year for Christmas, my friend Roxanne, who eats, sleeps, and dreams books, has given her mother books. Her mother, who is a macrame expert, has given her homemade crafts. On her mother's last visit, she inquired about where Roxanne had hung her latest craft gift, which was nowhere to be seen. Roxanne said, "Same place you put all the books I've given you: up in the attic." The two women laughed and agreed that this year they would stop trying to read each other's minds and then buy gifts based on their own interests. Instead, they'd spend more time learning about each other's passions and buy more thoughtful gifts that each other would want.

Following is a list of seventeen values. Number these values from 1 to 17, with 1 being most important and 17 being the least important. Ask your mother to do the same.

You	Mom	Value	Description
____	____	Art and beauty	Appreciation of the fine arts, culture, beauty
____	____	Competence	Being the best in some area
____	____	Creativity	Self-expression; using your imagination and resourcefulness to create
____	____	Environment	Acting as a steward for the planet
____	____	Gratitude	Appreciating and blessing life and all that you experience
____	____	Health	Taking care of your body; staying well
____	____	Independence	Doing things on your own; freedom to do as you believe
____	____	Learning	Accumulating knowledge and understanding of things that interest you
____	____	Pleasure	Being happy and having fun
____	____	Power	Controlling the situation around you
____	____	Relationships	Connection and intimacy with family, friends, community
____	____	Responsibility	Doing what's expected of you; following through on commitments

		Security	Feeling safe in the world; having enough money
____	____	Self-fulfillment	Developing your capacity, career; realizing your potential
____	____	Service	Contributing to the welfare of others
____	____	Spirituality	Devotion to your faith; connection to God or other higher power
____	____	Wealth	Earning a great deal of money

Once you have your lists, compare notes. You now know what is most important to each other. You can use this as a guideline for understanding differences, and for gift giving and acknowledgment. I have done this with families, couples, and work teams with great success. Here are a few examples:

- If your mother selected spirituality, you could go to church with her or buy her a new Bible.
- If security and wealth are important to her, instead of taking her to dinner, buy her a few shares of stock or join a women's investing club together.
- If service is important to her, offer to contribute money or time to the charity of her choice.

As much as we hope for someone else to read our minds and know exactly what we need, it often doesn't happen, and we experience disappointment. Let your mother know what motivates you. Tell your mother how she can appreciate you. Be willing to ask her what motivates her and how you can better appreciate her. You'll receive more of what you want in your life, and you'll feel more appreciative of yourself.

The Deepest Craving of the Human Spirit Is to Be Appreciated

Appreciation is one of the greatest gifts we give each other and ourselves. In my *Thanks! You Made My Day* programs on appreciation, when I ask people why they left their job, their marriage, or their birth family, it usually comes down to one answer: "I didn't feel appreciated." What do people want most in their life? William James, the father of modern psychology, said it as early as 1899: "The deepest craving of the human spirit is to be appreciated." Today we are no different. So why do we so often wait until someone dies before we express our appreciation?

Mom, You're the Real Hero in the Family

The phone rang at 2:40 A.M. I heard Jeanne's voice, "Mary? Mom's free now. She just took her last breath." "I'll be right there," I said. The ten-minute ride to my parents' house was filled with thoughts of regret, guilt, and sadness. I was exhausted after having left for my home at 10 P.M., kissing my mother good-bye, and saying, "I love you." I thought I felt her squeeze my hand ever so lightly. Why didn't I stay? I wanted to be there when she left her body. I had always felt strongly about not wanting to die alone and wanting someone I love to be holding my hand when I die. I wanted that experience with her. I was glad that Eileen and Jeanne were there, but I never asked Mom what she wanted.

The house was lit up when I got there. Mom was still warm, but beginning to cool. Her skin was an odd shade of cream with a glow that still shines in my mind's eye. I couldn't take my eyes off her and wondered if her spirit was hovering about.

After the hospice people had picked up my mother's body, our family sat around in the living room with dazed looks of shock on our faces. No one knew what to say. Jeanne spoke first: "You know how Mom loved to shop. We should bury her with her Boston Store charge card."

Eileen jumped in and said, "Yeah. Now Mom will be able to shop for-ever." My father was standing in the hallway and through choked tears said, "How dare you talk about your mother that way after she's just died. Show more respect for her!" We were all silent. The tension was high. Once again Jeanne broke through and said, "Dad, sometimes you have to laugh because if you don't, you'll cry and then you'll never stop. Dad said nothing, turned around, walked back into their bed-room, and closed the door. "Do not disturb" was written all over his body.

The following day we made funeral arrangements. Months earlier I had heard that performing an appreciation ritual at the funeral service would help assuage our grief. Each family member places a treasured memento of the person who has died into the casket and says a few words about the meaning of the memento. I mentioned this idea while we were discussing the agenda for the wake and church service. Dad said nothing, but my siblings all thought it was a good idea and agreed to bring something.

Our extended family of aunts, uncles, and cousins gathered the next morning at the funeral home for the closing of the casket and the fu-neral procession to the church and then to the grave site. As planned, Eileen, Paul, Jeanne, and I placed our mementos inside the casket. Jeanne put a toy truck my mother had given to her infant son, Michael, and said, "Mom, thank you for being a loving grandmother to Michael and spoiling him rotten. We love you." Paul put in a picture of his new little boy, Jimmy, who had been born the night before. He said, "Mom, I guess you met Jimmy on his way down here. Thanks for helping him arrive safely." I put a bottle of Mom's favorite nail polish (I bit my nails beyond the quick until I was in my twenties; when I finally stopped, she always told me how nice my hands looked) and an audiotape of my most recent speech, "Waking Up The Real You," and said, "Mom, thanks for always telling me I was beautiful inside and out. I dedicate the rest of my speaking career to you." Eileen gave Mom her Ironman Triathlon medal and said, "Mom, this is for dying with dignity and grace. You're the real hero in our family." As we turned around to leave, my father, who had been watching us, surprised us by walking up to the casket. He took something out of his pocket, slipped it into Mom's hand, and said, "Gracie, here's your Boston Store charge card. You always said, 'Shop until you drop.' Now you can do it forever. I love you."

My father's epiphany blessed our family with a moment of Grace—literally and figuratively. My mother's presence even in death brought light and joy. My only wish is that we had shared this appreciation with her when she was alive. You still have that opportunity. Take advantage of it. In the end, all that will matter is whom you loved and who loved you. Call your mother. She is a gift—and so are you!

Activities to Do with Your Mom

❑ Plan a surprise party for her birthday or Mother's Day.
❑ Make an audiotape or videotape of all the things you love about her, and give it to her for her birthday.
❑ Schedule a spa day, manicure, pedicure, or massage.
❑ Make her a scrapbook of photos and poems.
❑ Create a memory jar or memory box. (Visit *www.maryloverde.com* for a ready-made memory jar and blank cards.)
❑ Give her a service that will improve the quality of her life:
    Lawn mowing, snow plowing
    Grocery delivery, house cleaning
    Driving her to her doctor appointments
    A senior yoga or exercise class

Questions for Your Mom

• What is one of your happiest memories?
• What's one of the most meaningful gifts you've received?
• What's one of the most loving things someone has done for you?
• What's one of the most loving things you've ever done for someone?
• What music, poetry, art, books, or movies have most inspired you?
• What's your favorite place in nature?
• If you had six months left to live, how would you spend it?
• If this were your last day on earth, what would you do?

- You were right about . . .
- What are you most grateful for? Why? Count your blessings; name ten.
- What's one of the nicest things you've ever done for yourself?
- What's the best compliment anyone has ever paid you?
- What do you value most in yourself? What do you value most in me?
- What contribution to life are you most proud of?
- Three things I really appreciate about you, Mom, are . . .

EPILOGUE

In the nine years of living with my mother's quiet voice in my mind gently urging me to finish this book, many coincidences occurred that continue to astonish me. One incident in particular I am moved to tell you about because it reflects the wonderful gifts available to us when we listen with our heart and trust in divine guidance.

For several reasons I was reluctant to write this book. Exasperated after six years of doubt and resistance, I finally made an agreement with my mother's spirit and said, "Enough! I'll write this book if my story about us, 'Squeeze My Hand and I'll Tell You That I Love You,' is accepted in *Chicken Soup for the Mother's Soul.* If it's not, I'm letting this idea go and moving on with my life." I thought this was a good compromise because, with over 2,000 stories submitted and only 100 selected, I assumed it would take a miracle for my story to be published.

Nine months later, on April 11, 1997, I received a phone call from the Chicken Soup office; my story had been accepted. I sat at my desk in my office, amazed. *April 11 was the sixth anniversary of my mother's death.* I realized then that writing this book was not an option; it was a calling.

I have come to believe that on a spiritual level, this book fulfills a divine contract made between me and my mother to help me—and now you and your mother, and every other woman who passes through our lives—to know and feel deep in our beings that we are a gift to be respected, appreciated, and celebrated.

Thank you for sharing this journey. May you be blessed to recognize and carry out your divine contracts that are waiting to give you as much joy, fulfillment, and loving guidance as *My Mother, My Friend* has given me.

VALUABLE RESOURCES

For a current list of resources including books, magazines, news articles, Web sites, and support services, as well as further data on any research highlighted in *My Mother, My Friend*, or information on speaking engagements and consulting, please visit my Web site or contact me at one of the addresses listed below, and I'll be happy to send you more information.

I'd Love to Hear from You!

I welcome your stories, comments, questions; your mother's (or daughters') answers; and how you and your mother (or daughter) used the techniques and questions in this book!

Mary Marcdante

Please contact me at:
Web site: *http.//www.marymarcdante.com*
Email address: *Mary@marymarcdante.com*
Postal address: P.O. Box 2529, Del Mar, CA 92014

ABOUT THE AUTHOR

Mary Marcdante is a communication and stress management expert and professional speaker who works with people to help them discover their best, make healthier choices, and live their dreams. Her clients include Fortune 500 corporations, associations, educational institutions, communities, and women's health conferences. She has presented over fifteen hundred programs to organizations around the world, including the National Association for Women's Health, Kaiser Permanente, Hewlett Packard, Deloitte-Touche, and the Internal Revenue Service.

Mary Marcdante's work has been featured in media and print across the country, including *The Wall Street Journal*, *PM* magazine, *Chicago Tribune*, *Professional Speaker* magazine, and a nationally released image video sponsored by Burlington Sheer Indulgence. She was a grand prizewinner in the *Self* Magazine/Lady Foot Locker "Realize the Dream" contest. In addition to *My Mother, My Friend*, she is the author of *Inspiring Words for Inspiring People*, a contributing author to the bestselling *Chicken Soup for the Mother's Soul* and *Chicken Soup for the Pet Lover's Soul*, and *A Woman's Way to Success in Business*.

The author's experience also includes advertising, marketing, and image development. She was vice president of marketing and continuing education for a nationally recognized technology research firm. She has a B.F.A. degree in fashion design from Mount Mary College. Her graduate studies include psychology and art therapy. She has worked as a fashion stylist for top Midwest photographers and film and video producers. She is past president of the San Diego and Wisconsin chapters of the National Speakers Association and a member of the National Speakers Association and the National Association for Women's Health.

Mary Marcdante lives in Del Mar, California, and when not writing or speaking she can be found walking the coastline at Torrey Pines State Reserve Beach. For more information or to book her for a speaking engagement, email her at *Mary@marymarcdante.com* or write to her at P.O. Box 2529, Del Mar, CA 92014.